BACH'S CHORALS

BY

CHARLES SANFORD TERRY

PART I

THE HYMNS AND HYMN MELODIES

OF THE

"PASSIONS" AND ORATORIOS

Travis & Emery Music Bookshop

Charles Sanford Terry:

Bach's Chorals, Part I.

The Hymns and Hymn Melodies
of the
"Passions" and Oratorios.

Facsimile of 1915 edition.
First published Cambridge University Press 1915.
Republished Travis & Emery 2010.

Published by
Travis & Emery Music Bookshop
17 Cecil Court, London, WC2N 4EZ, United Kingdom.
(+44) 20 7240 2129
neworders@travis-and-emery.com

ISBN Hardback: 978-1-906857-25-7. Paperback: 978-1-906857-26-4

Charles Sanford Terry (1864-1936), Historian and Bach Scholar.

He studied at St. Pauls Cathedral Choir School as a solo boy, King's College and Lanc He studied history at Cambridge, He lectured in history at Durham College of Science an Aberdeen. He spent much of his life devoted to Music and to Bach in particular. He sta choral societies in both Newcastle and Durham. He wrote extensively on Bach. Wa Emery said that his biography of Bach was "the only one that is both detailed and readable

More details available from
· Stanley Sadie: The New Grove Dictionary of Music and Musicians.(Walter Emery).
· Dictionary of National Biography

Works:
Bach's B Minor Mass (1915)
Bach's Chorals (3 vols. 1915-1921, reprint Travis & Emery 2010)
Forkell (Translated C.S.T.): Johann Sebastian Bach: His Life, Art and Work. (1920)
J.S. Bach's Original Hymn-Tunes for Congregational Use (edited by Terry. 1922)
Bach: The Mass in B Minor (1924)
Bach: Coffee and Cupid (edited by C.S. Terry 1924)
Bach: The Cantatas and Oratorios (1925)
Bach: The Passions (1926).
Joh. Seb. Bach: Cantata Texts, sacred and Secular (1926, reprint Travis & Emery 2009)
Bach: a Biography (1928)
Bach: the Magnificat, Lutheran Masses and Motets (1929)
The Four Part Chorals of J.S. Bach (edited C.S.T. 1924, reprint Travis & Emery 2009)
The Origin of the Family of Bach Musicians (1929, reprint Travis & Emery 2009)
John Christian Bach (1929, reprint Travis & Emery 2009)
Bach: the Historical Approach (1930)
Bach's Orchestra (1932)
The Music of Bach (1933)

© Travis & Emery 2010.

BACH'S CHORALS

CAMBRIDGE UNIVERSITY PRESS
C. F. CLAY, Manager
London: FETTER LANE, E.C.
Edinburgh: 100 PRINCES STREET

New York: G. P. PUTNAM'S SONS
Bombay, Calcutta and Madras: MACMILLAN AND CO., Ltd.
Toronto: J. M. DENT AND SONS, Ltd.
Tokyo: THE MARUZEN-KABUSHIKI-KAISHA

All rights reserved

BACH'S CHORALS

BY

CHARLES SANFORD TERRY

PART I

THE HYMNS AND HYMN
MELODIES
OF THE
"PASSIONS" AND ORATORIOS

Cambridge :
at the University Press
1915

TO MY FRIEND
IVOR ATKINS

ERRATA

P. vi, lines 10–11, *delete* which...century
    line 13, *for* Johann Crüger *read* Paul Wagner

P. 13, line 8, *for* of 1552 *read* in 1552

PREFATORY NOTE

NO other country can vie with Germany in wealth of hymnody. Much of it was pre-Reformation in origin. Most of it was fruit of the spiritual exaltation of the Reformation and the Thirty Years' War. In its development the year 1524 is the starting-point—the "crucial year for German Church-music," Schweitzer calls it[1]. It witnessed the publication of the first German Hymn-Book, *Etlich Christlich lider Lobgesang, und Psalm* (Wittenberg, 1524), which contained eight hymns, set to four melodies. Another, *Eyn Enchiridion oder Handbuchlein...geystlicher gesenge und Psalmen, Rechtschaffen und kunstlich verteutscht*, was issued at Erfurt, and contained twenty-five hymns, set to sixteen melodies. In the same momentous year Johann Walther published at Wittenberg, under Luther's direction, his *Geystliche*

[1] Albert Schweitzer, *J. S. Bach* (1911), trans. Ernest Newman, vol. i. 15.

gesangk Buchleyn, which contained thirty-two hymns, and forty-three, mostly five-part, musical settings. Twenty-one years later (1545) Valentin Babst published at Leipzig his *Geystliche Lieder*, the last Hymn-Book that received Luther's revision. It contained one hundred and twenty-nine numbers and ninety-seven hymn melodies. Ninety-five years later Johann Crüger's *Newes vollkömliches Gesangbuch Augspurgischer Confession* (Berlin, 1640), which remained in use in Berlin for nearly a century, contained two hundred and forty-eight hymns and one hundred and thirty-five melodies. Johann Crüger's collection (1697)— Bach was twelve years old then—entitled *Andächtiger Seelen geistliches Brand- und Gantz-Opfer. Das ist vollständiges Gesangbuch in acht unterschiedlichen Theilen*, contained more than five thousand hymns, but no melodies. It is a work closely associated with Bach, who possessed the eight volumes and drew his hymns from them. Nearly one hundred years later (1786) an incomplete hymnological index of first lines revealed actually 72,733 German hymns! The *Dictionary of Hymnology* (1908) estimates that about 10,000 of them have become popular, of which "nearly one thousand are classical and immortal[1]." Bach

[1] P. 412.

drew lavishly upon this wealth of material, and for his choral works alone used 208 of the old melodies, of which he wrote actually 389 harmonisations, introducing the majority of them (204) into the "Passions," Oratorios, Cantatas, and Motetts. The remaining 185 were collected by Bach's son Karl Philipp Emmanuel (Leipzig, 4 Parts, 1784–87) and belonged, presumably, to works of his father which no longer are extant[1].

The Chorals annotated in the following pages occur in Bach's "Passions" and Oratorios, *i.e.* the "St Matthew Passion," the "St John Passion," the "Christmas Oratorio," and the "Ascension Oratorio," or Cantata, "Lobet Gott in seinen Reichen." The Easter Oratorio, or Cantata, "Kommt, eilet und laufet," contains no Chorals, and Bach was precluded from introducing them into the Masses and Magnificat[2]. These pages therefore exhaust the Choral material used by Bach outside the Cantatas, Motetts, Organ Preludes and Fantasias.

Throughout the four works Bach makes use altogether of forty old hymns or hymn-tunes: twelve for words and melody, eighteen for words only, ten for melody only. In three instances ("Christmas

---

[1] See *J. S. Bach's Werke*, VII, *Choralgesänge* (Breitkopf & Haertel), Vorwort (1898). The enumeration only includes Bach's simple, hymn-form, settings.

[2] But see p. 44.

Oratorio," Nos. 38, 40, 42) he uses a melody of his own.

The following twelve hymns provide both words and melody[1]:

* Christus der uns selig macht. 2, J.
  Ermuntre dich, mein schwacher Geist. 2, C, A.
*† Gelobet seist du, Jesu Christ. 2, C.
  Herzlich Lieb hab' ich dich, O Herr. 1, J.
  Herzliebster Jesu, was hast du verbrochen. 5, M, J.
*† In dich hab' ich gehoffet, Herr. 2, M, C.
*† O Lamm Gottes unschuldig. 1, M.
† Valet will ich dir geben. 1, J.
*† Vater unser im Himmelreich. 1, J.
*† Vom Himmel hoch da komm ich her. 3, C.
  Was mein Gott will, das g'scheh' allzeit. 1, M.
  Werde munter, mein Gemüthe. 1, M.

The following eighteen hymns provide their words only for the Chorals:

Befiehl du deine Wege. 1, M.
Du Lebensfürst, Herr Jesu Christ. 1, A.
Fröhlich soll mein Herze springen. 1, C.
Gott fähret auf gen Himmel. 1, A.
Hilf, Herr Jesu, lass gelingen. 1, C.
Ich steh' an deiner Krippen hier. 1, C.
Ihr Christen auserkoren. 1, C.

[1] The suffixed numeral indicates the number of times Bach uses the hymn or melody. The capital shows where he uses it; M and J standing for the two "Passions," C for the Christmas, and A for the Ascension Oratorio. A prefixed † indicates that Bach has illustrated the melody in his Organ Preludes, Variations, or Fantasias. A prefixed * indicates that the melody is treated in Bach's *Little Organ Book* (*Orgelbüchlein*).

Ihr Gestirn, ihr hohlen Lüfte. 1, C
Jesu, du mein liebstes Leben. 1, C.
Jesu Leiden, Pein und Tod. 3, J.
Lasst Furcht und Pein. 1, C.
Nun liebe Seel', nun ist es Zeit. 1, C.
O Haupt voll Blut und Wunden. 4, M.
O Mensch, bewein' dein Sünde gross. 1, M[1].
O Welt, sieh' hier dein Leben. 3, M, J.
Schaut! schaut! was ist für Wunder dar? 1, C.
Wie soll ich dich empfangen. 1, C.
Wir singen dir Immanuel. 1, C.

The following ten hymns provide their melody only for the Chorals:

* Es sind doch selig alle. 1, M[2].
Gott des Himmels und der Erden. 1, C.
† Herzlich thut mich verlangen. 7, M, C.
Jesu Kreuz, Leiden und Pein. 3, J.
Mach's mit mir, Gott, nach deiner Güt'. 1, J.
† Nun freut euch, lieben Christen g'mein. 1, C.
O Welt, ich muss dich lassen. 3, M, J.
*† Von Gott will ich nicht lassen. 1, A[3].
Warum sollt' ich mich denn grämen. 1, C.
*† Wir Christenleut'. 1, C.

Six hymns or their melodies occur in more than one of the "Passions" and Oratorios:

Ermuntre dich, mein schwacher Geist.
Herzlich thut mich verlangen.
Herzliebster Jesu, was hast du verbrochen.
In dich hab' ich gehoffet, Herr.

[1] Melody quoted as "Es sind doch selig alle."
[2] In the *Orgelbüchlein* as "O Mensch, bewein'."
[3] In the *Orgelbüchlein* as "Helft mir Gott's Güte preisen."

O Welt, ich muss dich lassen.
O Welt, sieh' hier dein Leben.

The words of the identified hymns are by the following seventeen writers, only one of whom, Gottfried Wilhelm Sacer, was Bach's contemporary:

Albrecht, Margrave of Brandenburg-Culmbach (1522–57).
Nicolaus Decius (d. 1541).
Johann Franck (1618–77).
Paul Gerhardt (1607–76).
Johann Heermann (1585–1647).
Valerius Herberger (1562–1627).
Sebald Heyden (d. 1561).
Martin Luther (1483–1546).
Adam Reissner, or Reusner (1496–c. 1575).
Johann Rist (1607–67).
Christoph Runge (1619–81).
Gottfried Wilhelm Sacer (1635–99).
Martin Schalling (1532–1608).
Paul Stockmann (1602?–36).
Michael Weisse (1480?–1534).
Georg Weissel (1590–1635).
Georg Werner (1589–1643).

Throughout the following pages the Bach-Gesellschaft hymn texts have been followed. They have been collated in every case with Carl E. P. Wackernagel's *Das deutsche Kirchenlied von der ältesten Zeit bis zu Anfang des XVII. Jahrhunderts* (Leipzig, 5 vols., 1864–77), or Albert Fischer's *Das deutsche evangelische Kirchenlied des siebzehnten Jahrhunderts vollendet und herausgegeben von D. W. Tümpel* (Gütersloh, 1904–). Verbal discrepancies between the original texts and Bach's versions are noted. The author of the stanza in the "St John Passion," No. 22, is not identified.

The non-anonymous melodies of the Chorals are, in addition to Bach himself, by the following fourteen composers, none of whom was Bach's contemporary:

> Heinrich Albert, or Alberti (1604–51).
> Seth Calvisius, or Kallwitz (1556–1615).
> Johann Crüger (1598–1662).
> Nicolaus Decius (d. 1541).
> Johann Georg Ebeling (1637–76).
> Caspar Fuger, or Füger, the younger (d. 1617).
> Matthäus Greitter (d. 1550 or 1552).
> Hans Leo Hassler (1564–1612).
> Heinrich Isaak (b. *circ.* 1440).
> Martin Luther (1483–1546).
> Johann Hermann Schein (1586–1630).
> Johann Schop, or Schopp (d. *circ.* 1665).
> Melchior Teschner (fl. 1613).
> Melchior Vulpius (1560?–1615).

In the following pages the melodies are printed in their earliest known form (see Johannes Zahn, *Die Melodien der deutschen evangelischen Kirchenlieder*, Gütersloh, 6 vols., 1889–93).

The composers of the following melodies cannot be identified:

i. *Was mein Gott will, das g'scheh' allzeit* ("St Matthew Passion," No. 31), whose secular parentage is not stated in Pierre Attaignant's volume, 1529.

ii. *Vater unser im Himmelreich* ("St John Passion," No. 5), published in 1539 and attributed to Luther.

iii. *Christus der uns selig macht* ("St John Passion," No. 12), the proper melody of "Patris Sapientia," first published by Michael Weisse in 1531.

iv. *Herzlich Lieb hab' ich dich, O Herr* ("St John Passion," No. 37), which was first published by Bernhard Schmidt in 1577.

v. *Gelobet seist du, Jesu Christ* ("Christmas Oratorio," No. 7), a pre-Reformation tune published, and probably moulded, by Johann Walther in 1524.

vi. *Vom Himmel hoch da komm ich her* ("Christmas Oratorio," No. 9), attributed to Luther.

vii. *Nun freut euch, lieben Christen g'mein* ("Christmas Oratorio," No. 59), attributed to Luther.

viii. *Von Gott will ich nicht lassen* ("Ascension Oratorio," No. 11), derived from a secular song extant in 1569.

On the origin of the melodies of the Reformation hymns the following passages of Schweitzer's *J. S. Bach* are illuminating:

"Since we rarely know the history of a melody before it became attached to a hymn, the name of which it henceforth bears, it is difficult to decide which melodies were adopted and which composed by the musicians of the Reformation....On the whole the number of musicians who wrote melodies for the Church was not large, not because at that time there were no musicians capable of the work, but rather because their services were not called for. For a new melody to become a true folk-melody, of the kind that would gain immediate xiii

acceptance everywhere, was a difficult process, requiring a long period of time. It was much more natural to impress existing melodies into the service of the Church, sacred melodies at first, and then, when these did not suffice, secular ones. The Reformed Church made the most abundant use of this latter source....For the Reformation it was a question of much more than acquiring serviceable melodies. While it brought the folk-song into religion, it wished to elevate secular art in general. That the object was conversion rather than simple borrowing is shown by the title of a collection that appeared at Frankfort in 1571 : 'Street songs, cavalier songs, mountain songs, transformed into Christian and moral songs, for the abolishing in course of time of the bad and vexatious practice of singing idle and shameful songs in the streets, in fields, and at home, by substituting for them good, sacred, honest words.'...Any foreign melody that had charm and beauty was stopped at the frontier and pressed into the service of the [Church].... When the treasures of melody to be drawn upon were at last exhausted, there came the epoch of the composer. The copious spiritual poetry of the seventeenth century called them to the work.... The spirit, however, which dominated music about the beginning of the eighteenth century made it incapable of developing the true church-tune any further. German music got out of touch with German song, and fell further and further under the influence of the more 'artistic' Italian melody. It could no longer achieve that naïveté which, ever since the Middle Ages, had endowed it with those splendid, unique tunes.... When Bach came on the scene, the great epoch of Choral creation was at an end, like that of the sacred poem. Sacred melodies indeed were still written; but they were songs of the Aria type, not true congregational hymns; an indefinable air of subjectivity pervaded them[1]."

Bach's Oratorios and "Passions" contain forty-three Chorals: fifteen in the "St Matthew Passion," twelve in the "St John Passion," fourteen in the "Christmas Oratorio," and two in the "Ascension Oratorio." Of that number the majority (33) are in simple hymn form suitable for congregational use. The remaining ten fall into four categories: (1) Nos. 9, 23, 42, 64 of the "Christmas Oratorio" may be termed Extended Chorals, the lines of the hymn being separated by orchestral interludes. (2) In No. 1 of the "St Matthew Passion" the Choral melody is woven into, independent of, and surges above the doubled chorus and orchestra below. (3) No. 25 of the "St Matthew Passion,"

[1] *Op. cit.* vol. i. 16-22.

No. 32 of the "St John Passion," and No. 7 of the "Christmas Oratorio" are alike in this: the hymn (set to a unison melody in the last of them) is part of a dialogue, either commenting upon the narrative of a solo voice, or, as in the "Christmas Oratorio," No. 7, providing the solo voice with the subject of its reflexions. (4) No. 35 of the "St Matthew Passion" and No. 11 of the "Ascension Oratorio" are Choral Fantasias, the Choral melody being woven into a complicated musical scheme. In the following pages the form and orchestration of every Choral are stated.

The author expresses his indebtedness to the Rev. James Mearns and his erudite articles on German hymnody in the *Dictionary of Hymnology*. He also cordially thanks his friend Mr Ernest Newman for reading this *opusculum* in proof, to its advantage. He dedicates it gratefully to another helper, most patient and skilled in Bach lore.

The author reserves for a second Part the Chorals of the Church Cantatas and Motetts.

KING'S COLLEGE,
OLD ABERDEEN.
October, 1915.

CONTENTS

	PAGE
Prefatory Note	v
The "St Matthew Passion"	1
The "St John Passion"	24
The "Christmas Oratorio"	41
The "Ascension Oratorio"	62

MELODIES

Christus, der uns selig macht (1531)	29
Ermuntre dich, mein schwacher Geist (1641)	45
Es sind doch selig alle (1525)	14
Gelobet seist du, Jesu Christ (1524)	42
Gott des Himmels und der Erden (1642)	57
Helft mir Gott's Güte preisen (1575 [1569])	63
Herzlich Lieb hab' ich dich, O Herr (1577)	38
Herzlich thut mich verlangen (1601)	8
Herzliebster Jesu, was hast du verbrochen (1640)	3
In dich hab' ich gehoffet, Herr (1581)	16
Jesu Kreuz, Leiden und Pein (1609)	27
Mach's mit mir, Gott, nach deiner Güt' (1628)	32
Nun freut euch, lieben Christen g'mein (1535)	58
O Lamm Gottes unschuldig (1542 and 1545)	1
O Welt, ich muss dich lassen (1539)	5
Valet will ich dir geben (1614)	34
Vater unser im Himmelreich (1539)	25
Vom Himmel hoch da komm ich her (1539)	44
Von Gott will ich nicht lassen (1572 [1571])	63
Warum sollt' ich mich denn grämen (1666)	49
Was mein Gott will, das g'scheh' allzeit (1529 and 1572 [1571])	12
Werde munter, mein Gemüthe (1642)	19
Wir Christenleut' (1593)	51
Index	66

THE ST MATTHEW PASSION
(1728—1729)

No. 1. O Lamb of God most holy (*O Lamm Gottes unschuldig*)[1]

Melody: "O Lamm Gottes unschuldig"

Nicolaus Decius 1542

Nicolaus Decius 1545

[1] The English titles are those in the Elgar-Atkins edition of the Oratorio, published by Novello & Co.

The melody, "O Lamm Gottes unschuldig," was composed or adapted by Nicolaus Decius (von Hofe or Hovesch) for his translation of the "Agnus Dei." Probably Decius was a native of Hof in Upper Franconia. In 1519 he became provost of the Cloister of Steterburg, near Wolfenbüttel, but, abjuring the Roman Catholic Church, was appointed master in the St Katharine and Egidien school at Brunswick in 1522. In 1526(?) he was instituted preacher in the Church of St Nicolas, Stettin. He died at Stettin in 1541, poisoned, it was suspected, by his Roman Catholic enemies. The tune was published, with the hymn, in Anton Corvinus' *Christliche Kirchen-Ordnung* (Erfurt, 1542), issued, with a Preface by Elisabeth Duchess of Brunswick-Lüneburg, for the use of the Principalities of Calenberg and Göttingen, of which she was Regent; and in Johann Spangenberg's *Kirchengesenge Deudtsch* (Magdeburg, 1545).

There is another harmonisation of the melody in the Bach *Choralgesänge*, No. 285.

The words of the Choral are the first stanza of Decius' translation of the "Agnus Dei qui tollis peccata mundi." It was first published in Low German in *Geystlyke leder*, Rostock, 1531, and in High German in Valentin S. Schumann's (d. 1545) *Geistliche lieder auffs new gebessert und gemehrt*, Leipzig, 1539:

NUMBER 3   3

O Lamm Gottes unschuldig,
Am Stamm des Kreuzes geschlachtet,
Allzeit erfund'n[1] geduldig,
Wiewohl du warest verachtet.
All' Sünd' hast du getragen,
Sonst müssten wir verzagen;
Erbarm' dich unser, O Jesu!   B.G. iv. 7.

English translations of the Hymn are noted in the *Dictionary of Hymnology*, pp. 31, 1550.

Form. The Choral (*Soprano ripieno*) is an independent strand or ornament of the Double Chorus (*Two Orchestras, each 2 Fl., 2 Ob., Strings, Organ, and Continuo*).

No. 3. O BLESSED JESU, HOW HAST THOU OFFENDED (*Herzliebster Jesu, was hast du verbrochen*)

Melody: "*Herzliebster Jesu*"   Johann Crüger 1640

The melody, "Herzliebster Jesu," composed for Heermann's Hymn by Johann Crüger, first

[1] 1539 gefunden.

appeared in his *Newes vollkömliches Gesangbuch*, Berlin, 1640. Crüger was born at Gross-Breesen, near Guben, in Brandenburg, in 1598. He became Cantor of St Nicolas' Church, Berlin, in 1622, and died in that city in 1662. About 20 of his melodies are still in common use, the most familiar of them being "Nun danket alle Gott."

Bach uses the melody elsewhere in the "St Matthew Passion" (Nos. 25, 55) and twice in the "St John Passion" (Nos. 4, 15).

The words of the Choral are the first stanza of the Passiontide Hymn, "Herzliebster Jesu, was hast du verbrochen." Its author, Johann Heermann, was born at Raudten, Silesia, in 1585. He became deacon of Köben on the Oder in 1611, retired in 1638, and died in 1647. The Hymn was first published in Heermann's *Devoti Musica Cordis. Hauss- und Hertz-Musica*, Leipzig, 1630; and, with a melody by Johann Staden (1581-1634), in the latter's *Hertzens Andachten*, 1631:

> Herzliebster Jesu, was hast du verbrochen,
> Dass man ein solch hart[1] Urtheil hat gesprochen?
> Was ist die Schuld, in was für Missethaten
> Bist du gerathen?   B.G. iv. 23.

English translations of the Hymn are noted in the *Dictionary of Hymnology*, pp. 517, 1648.

Form. Simple (*Flutes, Oboes, Strings, Organ, and Continuo*).

[1] 1630 scharff.

NO. 16. MY SIN IT IS WHICH BINDS THEE
(*Ich bin's, ich sollte büssen*)
Melody: "*O Welt, ich muss dich lassen*"
Heinrich Isaak 1539

Heinrich Isaak's melody was first published in Georg Forster's *Ein ausszug guter alter ūn newer Teutscher liedlein*, Nürnberg, 1539, but to the secular song, "Innsbruck, ich muss dich lassen." Of Isaak, Germany's first great composer, little is known. He was born *circ*. 1440, perhaps at Prague, was organist of the Medici chapel, Florence, 1477-93, and composer to the Emperor Maximilian I, 1496-1515. He died before 1531. The tune has survived through its association with Johann Hesse's (1490-1547) Hymn for the Dying, "O Welt, ich muss dich lassen," first published as a broadsheet at Nürnberg *circ*. 1555 and in the Nürnberg

Hymn-Book, *Geystliche Lieder, Psalmen und Lobgesenge. D. Mart. Luther*, Nürnberg, 1569. The words of Hesse's Hymn are a frank conversion of the travelling artisan's song, " Innsbruck, ich muss dich lassen," and the melody is styled " Innsbruck " in *Hymns Ancient and Modern* (No. 86). It was not until sixty years after its publication that Isaak's melody appeared in association with Hesse's Hymn. They were first published together in David Wolder's *New Catechismus Gesangbüchlein* (Hamburg, 1598 [1597]), and in the Eisleben *Gesangbuch, Darinnen Psalmen unnd Geistliche Lieder* (Eisleben, 1598). In the latter work the tune virtually assumed the form in which Bach employs it.

Bach uses the melody elsewhere in the " St Matthew Passion " (No. 44), and in the "St John Passion " (No. 8). He employs it also in three of the Cantatas : " Meine Seufzer, meine Thränen " (No. 13), for the Second Sunday after Epiphany ; " Sie werden euch in den Bann thun " (No. 44), for the Sixth Sunday after Easter ; and " In allen meinen Thaten " (No. 97), for general use. In the *Choralgesänge* there are four other harmonisations of the melody (Nos. 289, 290, 291, 298).

The words of the Choral are the fifth stanza of Paul Gerhardt's Passiontide Hymn, " O Welt, sieh' hier dein Leben," first published in the 1647 (Berlin) edition of Johann Crüger's *Praxis Pietatis Melica.* Paul Gerhardt was born in 1607, at Gräfenhainichen, near Wittenberg. At the age of fifty (1657) he became third deacon of the Church of St Nicolas, Berlin, during the reign of the Great Elector. For refusing to obey the Elector's order to treat with moderation the differences between the Calvinist and Lutheran Churches, Gerhardt was deposed in 1666. Three years later (1669) he became archdeacon at Lübben. He died in 1676. After Luther Gerhardt is the most popular of the German hymn-writers. He was the author of 120 hymns, which were collected and published in ten " Dozens " by Johann G. Ebeling (see the "Christmas Oratorio," No. 33), under the title *Pauli Gerhardi Geistliche Andachten* (Berlin, 1666–67):

> Ich bin's, ich sollte büssen,
> An Händen und an Füssen
> Gebunden in der Höll'.
> Die Geisseln und die Banden,
> Und was du ausgestanden,
> Das hat verdienet meine Seel'.
>
> B.G. iv. 42.

English translations of the Hymn are noted in the *Dictionary of Hymnology*, p. 853.

Form. Simple (2 *Ob.*, *Strings*, *Organ*, *and Continuo*).

8 ST MATTHEW PASSION

No. 21. RECEIVE ME, MY REDEEMER (*Erkenne mich, mein Hüter*)

Melody: "Herzlich thut mich verlangen"
Hans Leo Hassler 1601

Hans Leo Hassler's melody was published first in his *Lustgarten Neuer Teutscher Gesäng, Balletti, Galliarden und Intraden mit* 4, 5, 6 *und* 8 *Stimmen*, Nürnberg, 1601. It was, however, set there to a secular love song, "Mein G'müt ist mir verwirret von einer Jungfrau zart." Hassler, who was born at Nürnberg in 1564, studied music at Venice, and was organist and choirmaster at Nürnberg from 1601 to 1608. He was called to Dresden by the Electoral Prince in 1608, and died in his service in 1612. Like so many other secular tunes, Hassler's was pressed into the service of the Church. In 1613 it was attached to Christoph Knoll's (1563–1650) Hymn, "Herzlich thut mich verlangen" (*Harmoniae sacrae*, Görlitz, 1613), and forty-three years later, in Johann Crüger's *Praxis Pietatis Melica* (Frankfort, 1656), was set to Paul Gerhardt's "O Haupt voll Blut."

The melody is the principal one in the "St Matthew Passion" and is employed again in Nos. 23, 53, 63, and 72. Bach uses it also in the "Christmas Oratorio" (Nos. 5, 64), and in four of the Cantatas: "Ach Herr, mich armen Sünder" (No. 135), for the Third Sunday after Trinity; "Schau, lieber Gott, wie meine Feind'" (No. 153), for the Sunday after the Circumcision; "Sehet, wir geh'n hinauf nach Jerusalem" (No. 159), for Quinquagesima; and "Komm, du süsse Todesstunde!" (No. 161), for the Sixteenth Sunday after Trinity. There are other harmonisations of the tune in the *Choralgesänge*, Nos. 157, 158.

The words of the Choral are the fifth stanza of Paul Gerhardt's Passiontide Hymn, "O Haupt voll Blut," a translation of St Bernard of Clairvaulx' (?) "Salve caput cruentatum." It appeared first in Johann Crüger's *Praxis Pietatis Melica*, Frankfort, 1656. Other stanzas of the Hymn are used in Nos. 23, 63, and 72 *infra*:

> Erkenne mich, mein Hüter,
> Mein Hirte, nimm mich an,
> Von dir, Quell aller Güter,
> Ist mir viel Gut's gethan.
> Dein Mund hat mich gelabet
> Mit Milch und süsser Kost,
> Dein Geist hat mich begabet
> Mit mancher Himmelslust.
>   B.G. iv. 51.

English translations of the Hymn are noted in the *Dictionary of Hymnology*, pp. 835, 1681.

Form. Simple (2 *Fl.*, 2 *Ob.*, *Strings, Organ, and Continuo*).

NO. 23. HERE WOULD I STAND BESIDE THEE (*Ich will hier bei dir stehen*)

For Hans Hassler's melody, "Herzlich thut mich verlangen," see No. 21 *supra*.

The words of the Choral are the sixth stanza of Paul Gerhardt's Passiontide Hymn, "O Haupt voll Blut" (see No. 21):

> Ich will hier bei dir stehen:
> Verachte mich doch nicht!
> Von dir will ich nicht gehen,
> Wenn dir dein Herze bricht.
> Wann dein Herz wird erblassen
> Im letzten Todesstoss,
> Alsdann will ich dich fassen
> In meinen Arm und Schooss.
>
> B.G. iv. 53.

Form. Simple (2 *Ob.*, *Strings, Organ, and Continuo*).

NO. 25. MY SAVIOUR, WHY MUST ALL THIS ILL BEFALL THEE? (*Was ist die Ursach' aller solcher Plagen?*)

For Johann Crüger's melody, "Herzliebster Jesu," see No. 3 *supra*.

The words of the Choral are the third stanza of Johann Heermann's Passiontide Hymn, "Herzliebster Jesu, was hast du verbrochen" (see No. 3 *supra*):

> Was ist die Ursach' aller solcher Plagen[1]?
> Ach, meine Sünden haben dich geschlagen[2]!
> Ich, ach Herr Jesu, habe dies verschuldet,
> Was du erduldet!   B.G. iv. 55.

Form. The Choral (S.A.T.B.) is sung (*Strings, Organ, and Continuo*) in three detached phrases interrupting the Tenor *Recitativo* (2 *Fl.*, 2 *Ob. da caccia, Organ, and Continuo*).

No. 31. O FATHER, LET THY WILL BE DONE
(*Was mein Gott will*)

Melody: "*Il me souffit*"   Anon. 1529[3]

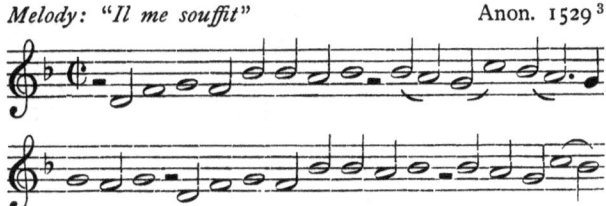

[1] 1630 Was ist doch wol die Ursach solcher Plagen?
[2] 1630 Ach Herr Jesu, ich hab dies wol verschuldet.
[3] Sung to the words of the French *chanson*:
> Il me souffit de tous mes maulx
> Puis qu'ils m'ont liure a mort.
> I'ay endure peine et trauaulx,
> Tant de douleur et desconfort.
> Que voules vous que ie vous face
> Pour estre en vostre grace?
> De douleur mon cœur si est mort
> Si ne voit vostre face.

12 ST MATTHEW PASSION

Melody: "Was mein Gott will"   Anon. 1572 [1571]

The melody, "Was mein Gott will," is of French origin, and was published first in Pierre Attaignant's *Trente et quatre chansons musicales* (Paris, [1529]), to the song "Il me souffit de tous mes maulx." It was sung in Antwerp in 1540 to Psalm cxl. It was attached to the Hymn, "Was mein Gott will," in Joachim Magdeburg's *Christliche und Tröstliche*

Tischgesenge, mit Vier Stimmen (Erfurt, 1572 [1571]). It appears to have been sung also to the secular song, "Beschaffens Glück ist unversaumt." Magdeburg was born *circ.* 1525 in the Altmark of Brandenburg. In 1549 he became pastor at Salzwedel in the Altmark, from whence he was banished upon his refusal to accept the Interim of 1552. After a wandering life he was living in Austria in 1583. The year of his death is not known.

Bach uses the melody elsewhere in six of the Cantatas: "Nimm, was dein ist, und gehe hin" (No. 144), for Septuagesima; "Alles nur nach Gottes Willen" (No. 72), for the Third Sunday after Epiphany; "Was mein Gott will" (No. 111), also for the Third Sunday after Epiphany; "Sie werden aus Saba Alle kommen" (No. 65), for Epiphany; "Ich hab' in Gottes Herz und Sinn" (No. 92), for Septuagesima; and "Ihr werdet weinen und heulen" (No. 103), for the Third Sunday after Easter.

The words of the Choral are the first stanza of Albrecht, Margrave of Brandenburg-Culmbach's only Hymn, "Was mein Gott will." He was born in 1522. As a soldier he gained for himself the name, "the German Alcibiades." Being a member of the Evangelical Union he was driven from Germany in 1554. He was permitted to return, and died in

ST MATTHEW PASSION

1557. The Hymn was first published as a broadsheet at Nürnberg *circ.* 1554, and in *Fünff Schöne Geistliche Lieder* (Dresden, 1556):

> Was mein Gott will, das g'scheh' allzeit,
> Sein Will' der ist der beste[1];
> Zu helfen den'n er ist bereit,
> Die an ihn glauben feste;
> Er hilft aus Noth,
> Der fromme Gott,
> Und züchtiget[2] mit Maassen.
> Wer Gott vertraut,
> Fest auf ihn baut,
> Den will er nicht verlassen.   B.G. iv. 83.

English translations of the Hymn are indicated in the *Dictionary of Hymnology*, p. 37.

Form. Simple (2 *Fl.*, 2 *Ob.*, *Strings, Organ, and Continuo*).

NO. 35. O MAN, THY GRIEVOUS SIN BEMOAN
(*O Mensch, bewein' dein' Sünde gross*)

Melody: "*Es sind doch selig alle*"   Matthäus Greitter 1525

[1] 1554 allerbeste.   [2] 1554 Er tröst die Welt.

The melody of "O Mensch, bewein'" most probably was composed by Matthäus Greitter. It was first published in the third Part of the *Teutsch Kirchëampt mit lobgsengen* (Strassburg, 1525; reprinted at Erfurt in 1848), and in *Psalmen, gebett und Kirchenübung wie sie zu Strassburg gehalten werden* (Strassburg, 1526), a book of 64 pp., containing 23 melodies, of which Greitter and his colleague Wolfgang Dachstein were the editors. In 1525–26 the melody was set to Greitter's version of Psalm cxix, "Es sind doch selig alle." In Calvin's Hymn-Book (Strassburg, 1539) it was adapted to Psalm xxxvi, "En moy le secret pensement." In the course of the sixteenth century it was sung to the Hymns, "Als Jesus Christus unser Herr" and "Komm, heilger Geist," and from *c.* 1584 chiefly to Heyden's "O Mensch, bewein'." Greitter was a monk and chorister of Strassburg Cathedral. He became a Protestant and in 1528 was assistant pastor of St Martin's Church, and later of St Stephen's Church, Strassburg. His death is dated variously as 1550 and 1552. Dachstein (d. *c.* 1561) was organist of St Thomas' Church, Strassburg, in the same period.

There is another harmonisation of the melody in the *Choralgesänge*, No. 286.

The words of the Choral are the first stanza of Sebald Heyden's Hymn, "O Mensch, bewein' dein' Sünde gross." Heyden was a native of Nürnberg

16   ST MATTHEW PASSION

and rector of the school attached to St Sebald's Church there. He died in 1561. The Hymn was first published as an 8-page (23 verses) broadsheet at Nürnberg, in 1525:

> O Mensch, bewein' dein' Sünde gross;
> Darum Christus sein's Vaters Schoos
> Äussert, und kam auf Erden.
> Von einer Jungfrau rein und zart
> Für uns er hie geboren ward,
> Er wollt' der Mittler werden.
> Den'n Todten er das Leben gab,
> Und legt' dabei all' Krankheit ab,
> Bis sich die Zeit herdrange,
> Dass er für uns geopfert würd',
> Trüg' unsrer Sünden schwere Bürd'
> Wohl an dem Kreuze lange.   B.G. iv. 107.

Form. Choral Fantasia (2 *Fl.*, 2 *Ob. d'amore, Strings, Organ, and Continuo*).

NO. 38. HOW FALSELY DOTH THE WORLD ACCUSE! (*Mir hat die Welt trüglich gericht't*)
Melody: "*In dich hab' ich gehoffet, Herr*"
Seth Calvisius 1581

The melody, "In dich hab' ich gehoffet, Herr," was composed by Seth Calvisius (Kallwitz). He was born at Gorsleben (Thuringia) in 1556, and became Cantor of St Thomas' Church, Leipzig, in 1594. He died in 1615. The melody was first published by the Augsburg preacher Gregorius Sunderreitter in his Psalter, *Davids Himlische Harpffen von neuwem auffgezogen* (Nürnberg, 1581), a revision of his Augsburg *Psalterium* of 1574. It was there associated with Reissner's Hymn, and again in Calvisius's *Hymni sacri Latini et germanici* (Erfurt, 1594). By 1627 (Schein's *Cantional*) the melody had assumed the form, to a great extent, in which Bach uses it.

Bach uses the melody elsewhere in the "Christmas Oratorio" (No. 46), and in the Cantatas, "Falsche Welt, dir trau ich nicht" (No. 52), for the Twenty-third Sunday after Trinity; and "Gottes Zeit ist die allerbeste Zeit" (No. 106, the *Actus Tragicus*).

The words of the Choral are the fifth stanza of Adam Reissner's, or Reusner's, Hymn (based on Psalm xxxi), "In dich hab' ich gehoffet, Herr," which was first published in *Form und Ordnung Gaystlicher Gesang und Psalmen*, Augsburg, 1533. Adam Reissner was born at Mindelheim in Swabian Bavaria in 1496. He fought in the Italian campaign, 1526–27, and was present at the sack of

18 ST MATTHEW PASSION

Rome in the latter year. He died at Mindelheim *circ.* 1575:

>Mir hat die Welt trüglich gericht't
>Mit Lügen und mit falschem G'dicht[1],
>Viel Netz und heimlich Strikken.
>Herr, nimm mein wahr
>In dieser G'fahr,
>B'hüt' mich vor falschen Tükken. B.G. iv. 151.

Translations of Reissner's Hymn are noted on page 955 of the *Dictionary of Hymnology*.

Form. Simple (2 *Fl.*, 2 *Ob.*, *Strings, Organ, and Continuo*).

NO. 44. O LORD, WHO DARES TO SMITE THEE?
(*Wer hat dich so geschlagen*)

For Heinrich Isaak's melody, "O Welt, ich muss dich lassen," see No. 16 *supra*.

The words of the Choral are the third stanza of Paul Gerhardt's Passiontide Hymn, "O Welt, sieh' hier dein Leben" (see No. 16):

>Wer hat dich so geschlagen,
>Mein Heil, und dich mit Plagen
>So übel zugericht?
>Du bist ja nicht ein Sünder,
>Wie wir und unsre Kinder;
>Von Missethaten[2] weisst du nicht.
>   B.G. iv. 164.

Form. Simple (2 *Fl.*, 2 *Ob.*, *Strings, Organ, and Continuo*).

---

[1] 1533 dicht.   [2] 1647 Ubelthaten.

No. 48. LAMB OF GOD, I FALL BEFORE THEE
(*Bin ich gleich von dir gewichen*)

Melody: "*Werde munter, mein Gemüthe*"
Johann Schop 1642

The melody, "Werde munter, mein Gemüthe," was composed by Johann Schop, or Schopp. The date of his birth is not ascertained. He was a talented instrumentalist, and, after a career at Wolfenbüttel and the Danish Court, became (1621) Director of the Ratsmusik, and later, Town Organist, and organist of the Church of St James, at Hamburg. He died about 1664 or 1665. The tune was first published, with the hymn, in Johann Rist's *Himlischer Lieder mit Melodeien*, Lüneburg, 1642.

Bach has used the melody elsewhere in four of the Cantatas: " Wir müssen durch viel Trübsal in das Reich Gottes eingehen" (No 146), for the Third Sunday after Easter; "Ich armer Mensch, ich Sündenknecht" (No. 55), for the Twenty-second Sunday after Trinity; "Mein liebster Jesus ist verloren" (No. 154), for the First Sunday after Epiphany; and "Herz und Mund und That und Leben" (No. 147), for the Feast of the Visitation of the B. V. M. There are two other harmonisations of the tune in the *Choralgesänge*, Nos. 363, 364.

The words of the Choral are the sixth stanza of Johann Rist's Evening Hymn, "Werde munter, mein Gemüthe," which was first published in the third Part of Rist's *Himlischer Lieder*, Lüneburg, 1642. Rist, a most prolific hymn-writer, was born at Ottensen, near Hamburg, in 1607. He was educated at Rostock and in 1635 became pastor at Wedel, near Hamburg. He died in 1667:

Bin ich gleich von dir gewichen,
Stell' ich mich doch wieder ein;
Hat uns doch dein Sohn verglichen
Durch sein' Angst und Todespein.
Ich verleugne nicht die Schuld,
Aber deine Gnad' und Huld
Ist viel grösser als die Sünde,
Die ich stets in mir befinde.
B.G. iv. 173.

Translations of the Hymn into English are noted in the *Dictionary of Hymnology*, p. 1254.

Form. Simple (2 *Fl.*, 2 *Ob.*, *Strings*, *Organ*, and *Continuo*).

No. 53. COMMIT THY WAY TO JESUS (*Befiehl du deine Wege*)

For Hans Hassler's melody, "Herzlich thut mich verlangen," see No. 21 *supra*.

The words of the Choral are the first stanza of Paul Gerhardt's (see No. 16) Hymn, "Befiehl du deine Wege," which was first published in Johann Crüger's *Praxis Pietatis Melica*, Frankfort, 1656. The Hymn is an acrostic, formed by the initial words of the stanzas, on Luther's version of Psalm xxxvii. 5: "Befiehl dem Herren deine Wege und hoffe auf ihn, er wirds wohl machen":

> Befiehl du deine Wege
> Und was dein Herze kränkt
> Der allertreusten Pflege
> Dess, der den Himmel lenkt;
> Der Wolken, Luft und Winden
> Giebt Wege, Lauf und Bahn,
> Der wird auch Wege finden,
> Da dein Fuss gehen kann. B.G. iv. 186.

Translations of the Hymn into English are noted on p. 125 of the *Dictionary of Hymnology*.

Form. Simple (2 *Fl.*, 2 *Ob.*, *Strings, Organ, and Continuo*).

No. 55. O WONDROUS LOVE, THAT SUFFERS THIS CORRECTION! (*Wie wunderbarlich ist doch diese Strafe!*)

For Johann Crüger's melody, "Herzliebster Jesu," see No. 3 *supra*.

The words of the Choral are the fourth stanza of Johann Heermann's Passiontide Hymn, "Herzliebster Jesu" (see No. 3):

<blockquote>
Wie wunderbarlich ist doch diese Strafe!
Der gute Hirte leidet für die Schaafe;
Die Schuld bezahlt der Herre, der Gerechte,
Für seine Knechte!   B.G. iv. 192.
</blockquote>

Form. Simple (2 *Fl.*, 2 *Ob.*, *Strings, Organ, and Continuo*).

No. 63. O SACRED HEAD, SURROUNDED (*O Haupt voll Blut*)

For Hans Hassler's melody, "Herzlich thut mich verlangen," see No. 21 *supra*.

The words of the Choral are the first and second stanzas of Paul Gerhardt's Passiontide Hymn, "O Haupt voll Blut" (see No. 21):

<blockquote>
O Haupt voll Blut und Wunden,
Voll Schmerz und voller Hohn!
O Haupt, zu Spott gebunden
Mit einer Dornenkron'!
O Haupt, sonst schön gezieret
Mit höchster Ehr' und Zier,
Jetzt aber hoch schimpfiret:
Gegrüsset seist du mir!

Du edles Angesichte,
Vor dem sonst schrickt und scheut
Das grosse Weltgerichte[1],
Wie bist du so bespeit!
</blockquote>

[1] 1656 Weltgenrichte.

Wie bist du so erbleichet,
Wer hat dein Augenlicht,
Dem sonst kein Licht nicht gleichet,
So schändlich zugericht't?
B.G. iv. 214.

Form. Simple (2 *Fl.*, 2 *Ob.*, *Strings, Organ, and Continuo*).

No. 72. BE NEAR ME, LORD, WHEN DYING
(*Wenn ich einmal soll scheiden*)

For Hans Hassler's melody, "Herzlich thut mich verlangen," see No. 21 *supra*.

The words of the Choral are the ninth stanza of Paul Gerhardt's Passiontide Hymn, "O Haupt voll Blut" (see No. 21):

Wenn ich einmal soll scheiden,
So scheide nicht[1] von mir!
Wenn ich den Tod soll leiden,
So tritt du dann herfür!
Wenn mir am allerbängsten
Wird um das Herze sein,
So reiss mich aus den Aengsten
Kraft deiner Angst und Pein!
B.G. iv. 248.

Form. Simple (2 *Fl.*, 2 *Ob.*, *Strings, Organ, and Continuo*)[2].

[1] 1656 mich.
[2] B.G. xli. 201 prints the original closing Choral of Part I of the Oratorio, the sixth and last stanza of Christian Keimann's (1607–62) Hymn, "Meinen Jesum lass ich nicht." The melody is Andreas Hammerschmidt's (1612–75). It is No. 247 of the *Choralgesänge*.

THE ST JOHN PASSION
(1723)

No. 4[1]. O WONDROUS LOVE (*O grosse Lieb'*)[2]

For Johann Crüger's melody, "Herzliebster Jesu, was hast du verbrochen," see "St Matthew Passion," No. 3.

The words of the Choral are the seventh stanza of Johann Heermann's Passiontide Hymn, "Herzliebster Jesu, was hast du verbrochen" (see "St Matthew Passion," No. 3). Two more stanzas of the Hymn are sung in No. 15 *infra*:

> O grosse Lieb', O Lieb' ohn' alle Maasse,
> Die dich gebracht auf diese Marter-Strasse!
> Ich lebte mit der Welt in Lust und Freuden,
> Und du musst leiden!
>
> B.G. xii. (1) 17.

Form. Simple (2 *Fl.*, 2 *Ob.*, *Strings, Organ, and Continuo*).

---

[1] No. 7 in Peters' edition.

[2] The English titles are those of the Rev. J. Troutbeck's version, published by Novello & Co.

NUMBERS 4 AND 5

No. 5[1]. THY WILL, O LORD, BE DONE
(*Dein Will' gescheh'*)

Melody: "*Vater unser im Himmelreich*"   Anon. 1539

The melody, "Vater unser im Himmelreich," by an unknown composer, appeared first in Valentin S. Schumann's (d. 1545) *Geistliche lieder auffs new gebessert*, Leipzig, 1539. The tune has been attributed to Luther, but on inadequate evidence.

Bach uses the melody elsewhere in three of the Cantatas: "Nimm von uns, Herr, du treuer Gott" (No. 101), for the Tenth Sunday after Trinity; "Es reifet euch ein schrecklich Ende" (No. 90), for the Twenty-fifth Sunday after Trinity; and "Herr, deine Augen sehen nach dem Glauben" (No. 102), for the Tenth Sunday after Trinity. There is

---
[1] No. 9, Peters' edition.

26 ST JOHN PASSION

another harmonisation of the tune in the *Choralgesänge*, No. 316, which Bach used for the earlier performances of the "St John Passion."

The words of the Choral are the fourth stanza of Luther's versification of the Lord's Prayer, which was first published, with the tune, in Valentin S. Schumann's *Geistliche lieder*, Leipzig, 1539:

> Dein Will' gescheh', Herr Gott, zugleich
> Auf Erden wie im Himmelreich;
> Gieb uns Geduld in Leidenszeit,
> Gehorsamsein in Lieb' und Leid,
> Wehr' und steur' allem Fleisch und Blut,
> Das wider deinen Willen thut.
> B.G. xii. (1) 18.

English translations of the Hymn are noted in the *Dictionary of Hymnology*, p. 1205.

Form. Simple (2 *Fl.*, 2 *Ob.*, *Strings*, *Organ*, and *Continuo*).

No. 8[1]. O LORD, WHO DARES TO SMITE THEE?
(*Wer hat dich so geschlagen*)

For Heinrich Isaak's melody, "O Welt, ich muss dich lassen," see the "St Matthew Passion," No. 16.

The words of the Choral are the third and fourth stanzas of Paul Gerhardt's Passiontide Hymn, "O Welt, sieh' hier dein Leben" (see the

[1] No. 15, Peters' edition.

"St Matthew Passion," No. 16. Stanza iii. is used by Bach also in No. 44 there):

> Wer hat dich so geschlagen,
> Mein Heil, und dich mit Plagen
> So übel zugericht't?
> Du bist ja nicht ein Sünder,
> Wie wir und unsre Kinder,
> Von Missethaten[1] weisst du nicht.
>
> Ich, ich und meine Sünden,
> Die sich wie Körnlein finden
> Des Sandes an dem Meer,
> Die haben dir erreget
> Das Elend, das dich schläget,
> Und das betrübte Marterheer.
>
> B.G. xii. (1) 31.

Form. Simple (2 *Fl.*, 2 *Ob.*, *Strings, Organ, and Continuo*).

No. 11[2]. PETER, FAITHLESS, THRICE DENIES
(*Petrus, der nicht denkt zurück*)

Melody: "*Jesu Kreuz, Leiden und Pein*"

Melchior Vulpius 1609

* *sic.*

[1] 1647 Ubelthaten.   [2] No. 20, Peters' edition.

The melody, "Jesu Kreuz, Leiden und Pein," was composed by Melchior Vulpius. He was born at Wasungen *circ.* 1560 and became Cantor at Weimar *circ.* 1596. He died there in 1615. This, his most notable, tune appeared in his *Ein schön geistlich Gesangbuch*, published at Jena in 1609, an enlarged edition of his *Kirchen Geseng und Geistliche Lieder*, Leipzig, 1604. It is there set to Petrus Herbert's (d. 1571) Hymn "Jesu Kreuz, Leiden und Pein." Adjusted to Paul Stockmann's "Jesu Leiden, Pein und Tod," it was included in Johann Hildebrandt's *Geistlicher Zeit-Vertreiber* (Leipzig, 1656). By 1714 (the Weissenfels *Gesang-Und Kirchenbuch*) the tune had in great measure assumed the form Bach employs.

The melody may be regarded as the principal one of the "St John Passion," where it appears again in Nos. 30 and 32. Bach uses it also in the Cantatas "Sehet, wir geh'n hinauf nach Jerusalem" (No. 159), for Quinquagesima; and "Himmelskönig, sei willkommen" (No. 182), for Palm Sunday.

The words of the Choral are the tenth stanza of Paul Stockmann's Passiontide Hymn, "Jesu Leiden, Pein und Tod," which first appeared in his *Aller Christen Leib-Stücke*, Leipzig, 1633. Stockmann was born at Lauchstädt in 1602 or 1603. He served under Gustavus Adolphus of Sweden as a Lutheran field preacher, and after residing at

Wittenberg and Leipzig, became pastor of Lützen. He died there in 1636:

> Petrus, der nicht denkt zurück,
> Seinen Gott verneinet,
> Der doch auf ein'n ernsten Blick
> Bitterlichen weinet:
> Jesu, blicke mich auch an,
> Wenn ich nicht will büssen;
> Wenn ich Böses hab' gethan,
> Rühre mein Gewissen.
> B.G. xii. (1) 39.

Form. Simple (2 *Fl.*, 2 *Ob.*, *Strings, Organ, and Continuo*).

No. 12[1]. SEE THE LORD OF LIFE AND LIGHT
(*Christus, der uns selig macht*)
Melody: "*Christus, der uns selig macht*"
"Patris Sapientia" 1531

---
[1] No. 21, Peters' edition.

ST JOHN PASSION

The melody, "Christus, der uns selig macht," proper to the Latin hymn "Patris Sapientia," was first published by Michael Weisse in the earliest German Hymn-Book of the Bohemian Brethren, *Ein New Gesengbuchlen*, Jung Bunzlau, 1531. With slight variations Bach uses one of his predecessors', Calvisius, version of the melody, published in his *Harmonia Cantionum ecclesiasticarum* (1598). Michael Weisse was born *circ.* 1480 at Neisse in Silesia. He became a monk at Breslau, adopted Lutheranism, entered the Bohemian Brethren's House at Leutomischl, and acted as their preacher in Bohemia and Moravia. He also edited their *Gesengbuchlen* of 1531. He died in 1534.

Bach uses the melody elsewhere in the "St John Passion" (No. 35). There is another harmonisation of it in the *Choralgesänge*, No. 48.

The words of the Choral are the first stanza of Michael Weisse's Passiontide Hymn, "Christus, der uns selig macht," a free translation of the Latin "Patris sapientia, veritas divina." It was first published, with the tune, in *Ein New Gesengbuchlen* of 1531, which contained 157 hymns written or translated by Weisse himself:

Christus, der uns selig macht,
Kein Bös's hat begangen,
Der ward für uns in der Nacht[1]
Als ein Dieb gefangen,

[1] 1531 Wart für uns zur Mitternacht.

Geführt vor gottlose Leut'
Und fälschlich verklaget,
Verlacht, verhöhnt und verspeit,
Wie denn die Schrift saget.
B.G. xii. (1) 43.

Translations of the Hymn into English are noted in the *Dictionary of Hymnology*, p. 886.

Form. Simple (2 *Fl.*, 2 *Ob.*, *Strings, Organ, and Continuo*).

NO. 15[1]. O MIGHTY KING (*Ach, grosser König*)

For Johann Crüger's melody, "Herzliebster Jesu," see the "St Matthew Passion," No. 3.

The words of the Choral are the eighth and ninth stanzas of Johann Heermann's Passiontide Hymn, "Herzliebster Jesu, was hast du verbrochen" (see the "St Matthew Passion," No. 3):

Ach, grosser König, gross zu allen Zeiten,
Wie kann ich g'nugsam diese Treu' ausbreiten?
Kein's Menschen Herze mag indess ausdenken[2],
Was dir zu schenken.

Ich kann's mit meinen Sinnen nicht erreichen,
Womit doch dein Erbarmen zu vergleichen.
Wie kann ich dir denn deine Liebesthaten
Im Werk erstatten?
B.G. xii. (1) 52.

Form. Simple (2 *Fl.*, 2 *Ob.*, *Strings, Organ, and Continuo*).

[1] No. 27, Peters' edition.
[2] 1630 vermag es auszudenken.

32 ST JOHN PASSION

No. 22[1]. THY BONDS, O SON OF GOD MOST HIGH
(*Durch dein Gefängniss, Gottes Sohn*)
Melody: "*Mach's mit mir, Gott, nach deiner Güt'*"
Johann Hermann Schein 1628

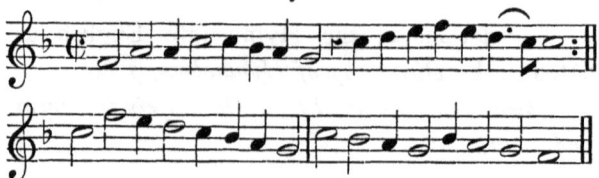

The melody and Hymn, " Mach's mit mir, Gott, nach deiner Güt'," composed and written by Johann Hermann Schein, were first published together in broadsheet form (Leipzig, 1628) as a " Trost-Liedlein " for five voices. The melody and Hymn (stanzas i.–v.) were included in Schein's *Cantional Oder Gesang-Buch Augsburgischer Confession*, of which the second edition was published at Leipzig in 1645 (first edition, 1627). The melody is generally known as " Eisenach."

Schein was born at Grünhain, Saxony, in 1586. In 1616, having recently been appointed Kapellmeister at the ducal court of Saxe-Weimar, he succeeded Seth Calvisius as Cantor of St Thomas' Church, Leipzig. He held the post until his death in 1630, and was one of the most distinguished musicians of the period. Of the 237 Choral melodies in his *Cantional*, 81 are by him.

[1] No. 40, Peters' edition.

Bach uses the melody elsewhere in the Cantatas, "Wohl dem, der sich auf seinen Gott" (No. 139), for the Twenty-third Sunday after Trinity; and "Ich steh' mit einem Fuss im Grabe" (No. 156), for the Third Sunday after Epiphany. There is another harmonisation of the tune in the *Choralgesänge*, No. 237.

The words of the Choral are from an unknown source. Their workmanship does not suggest the "delicate unknown poet" who revised Brockes' text of the "Passion" for Bach, whom Schweitzer (vol. ii. 175) conjectures to be the author of the text of the Cantatas "Sie werden aus Saba Alle kommen" (No. 65), "Mein liebster Jesu ist verloren" (No. 154), and "Du wahrer Gott und Davidssohn" (No. 23). The stanza is discoverable neither in Brockes' libretto (set to music by Handel and others), nor in the 1697 (Leipzig) eight-volumed Hymn-Book, from which Bach chiefly drew his Choral texts:

> Durch dein Gefängniss, Gottes Sohn,
> Ist uns die Freiheit kommen,
> Dein Kerker ist der Gnadenthron,
> Die Freistatt aller Frommen;
> Denn gingst du nicht die Knechtschaft ein,
> Müsst' unsre Knechtschaft ewig sein.
>   B.G. xii. (1) 74.

Form. Simple (2 *Fl.*, 2 *Ob.*, *Strings, Organ, and Continuo*).

No. 28[1]. WITHIN OUR INMOST BEING (*In meines Herzens Grunde*)

Melody: "Valet will ich dir geben"

Melchior Teschner 1614

The melody, "Valet will ich dir geben," composed by Melchior Teschner, was first published, along with the words of Valerius Herberger's Hymn (see *infra*), as a broadsheet, at Leipzig, in 1614. A second melody was printed in the broadsheet, also by Teschner, which has fallen out of use. The surviving melody is familiar in *Hymns Ancient and Modern* as "St Theodulph," No. 98. It bears a striking resemblance to the air of the anonymous 16th century "Sellenger's Round" (see Grove iv. 409). But Teschner's authorship is attested as early as 1656 (Johann Hildebrandt's *Geistlicher Zeit-Vertreiber*, Leipzig, 1656). Of Melchior Teschner little is known beyond the fact that he was Lutheran Cantor at Fraustadt, Silesia, early in the seventeenth century.

---

[1] No. 52, Peters' edition.

NUMBER 28

Bach uses the melody in the Cantata "Christus, der ist mein Leben" (No. 95), for the Sixteenth Sunday after Trinity. There is another harmonisation of the tune in the *Choralgesänge*, No. 314.

The words of the Choral are the third stanza of Valerius Herberger's Hymn for the Dying, "Valet will ich dir geben." It was written during the Silesian plague in 1613, appeared first as a broadsheet (see *supra*) in 1614, and later in the Gotha *Cantionale sacrum* of 1648, whence it passed into common use. Valerius Herberger was born at Fraustadt in 1562. In 1590 he became deacon and in 1599 chief pastor of St Mary's Church, Fraustadt, where Teschner was Cantor. Ejected in 1604 as a Lutheran, Herberger on Christmas Eve opened a meeting-house at Fraustadt, the "Kripplein Christi." He died in 1627. The Hymn is an acrostic on his name, Valerius, formed by the initial "Vale" of stanza i. and the initial letter of the opening line of the following four stanzas:

> In meines Herzens Grunde,
> Dein Nam' und Kreuz allein
> Funkelt allzeit und Stunde,
> Drauf kann ich fröhlich sein.
> Erschein' mir in dem Bilde
> Zu Trost in meiner Noth,
> Wie du, Herr Christ, so milde
> Dich hast geblut't zu Tod.   B.G. xii. (1) 95.

English translations of the Hymn are noted in the *Dictionary of Hymnology*, p. 511.

Form. Simple (2 *Fl.*, 2 *Ob.*, *Strings*, *Organ*, and *Continuo*).

No. 30[1]. WHILE HIS PARTING SPIRIT SINKS
(*Er nahm Alles wohl in Acht*)

For Melchior Vulpius' melody, "Jesu Kreuz, Leiden und Pein," see No. 11 *supra*.

The words of the Choral are the twentieth stanza of Paul Stockmann's Passiontide Hymn, "Jesu Leiden, Pein und Tod" (see No. 11):

> Er nahm Alles wohl in Acht
> In der letzten Stunde,
> Seine Mutter noch bedacht',
> Setzt ihr ein'n Vormunde.
> O Mensch, mache Richtigkeit,
> Gott und Menschen liebe,
> Stirb darauf ohn' alles Leid,
> Und dich nicht betrübe!
>
> B.G. xii. (1) 103.

Form. Simple (2 *Fl.*, 2 *Ob.*, *Strings*, *Organ*, and *Continuo*).

---

[1] No. 56, Peters' edition.

No. 32[1]. Jesu, thou who knewest death
(*Jesu, der du warest todt*)

For Melchior Vulpius' melody, "Jesu Kreuz, Leiden und Pein," see No. 11 *supra*.

The words of the Choral are the thirty-fourth stanza of Paul Stockmann's Passiontide Hymn, "Jesu Leiden, Pein und Tod" (see No. 11):

> Jesu, der du warest todt,
> Lebest nun ohn' Ende,
> In der letzten Todesnoth
> Nirgend mich hinwende[2]
> Als zu dir, der mich versühnt.
> O mein trauter Herre!
> Gieb mir nur, was du verdient,
> Mehr ich nicht begehre.
>
> B.G. xii. (1) 108.

Form. The Choral (S.A.T.B.) is sung in eight detached phrases accompanying the Bass *Aria* (*Organ and Continuo*).

No. 35[3]. Help us, Christ, Almighty Son
(*O hilf, Christe, Gottes Sohn*)

For the melody, "Christus, der uns selig macht," see No. 12 *supra*.

---

[1] No. 60, Peters' edition.   [2] 1633 hin mich wende.
[3] No. 65, Peters' edition.

38 ST JOHN PASSION

The words of the Choral are the eighth stanza of Michael Weisse's Passiontide Hymn, "Christus, der uns selig macht" (see No. 12):

> O hilf, Christe, Gottes Sohn,
> Durch dein bittres Leiden,
> Dass wir, dir stets unterthan,
> All' Untugend meiden;
> Deinen Tod und sein' Ursach'
> Fruchtbarlich bedenken,
> Dafür, wiewohl arm und schwach,
> Dir Dankopfer schenken.
>
> B.G. xii. (1) 121.

Form. Simple (2 *Fl.*, 2 *Ob.*, *Strings, Organ, and Continuo*).

No. 37[1]. LORD JESUS, THY DEAR ANGEL SEND
(*Ach Herr, lass dein lieb' Engelein*)

Melody: "*Herzlich Lieb hab' ich dich, O Herr*"

Anon. 1577

[1] No. 68, Peters' edition.

The melody, "Herzlich Lieb hab' ich dich, O Herr," was first published in Bernhard Schmidt's *Zwey Bücher Einer Neuen Kunstlichen Tabulatur auf Orgel und Instrument*, Strassburg, 1577. In Paschasius Reinigius' *Haus Kirchen Cantorei* (Bautzen, 1587) it is associated with a Tenor, which moves almost uniformly in sixths below Schmidt's treble, and is treated as the melody in *Geistlich Kleinod* (Leipzig, 1586).

The melody is used elsewhere by Bach in two of the Cantatas: "Man singet mit Freuden vom Sieg" (No. 149), for Michaelmas; and "Ich liebe den Höchsten" (No. 174), for Whitsuntide. There is another harmonisation of the tune in the *Choralgesänge*, No. 152.

The words of the Choral are the third stanza of Martin Schalling's only known Hymn, "Herzlich Lieb hab' ich dich, O Herr" (for the Dying). The Hymn was written *circ.* 1567 and was first published, with the germ of the melody, in *Newe Symbola etlicher Fürsten*, Nürnberg, 1571. Schalling was born at Strassburg in 1532, educated at Wittenberg University, and in 1554 became deacon at Regensburg. Later he settled at Amberg in Bavaria, and was appointed General-Superintendent of the Bavarian Oberpfalz. In 1585 he became pastor of St Mary's Church, Nürnberg. He died at Nürnberg in 1608:

40 ST JOHN PASSION

    Ach Herr, lass dein lieb' Engelein
    Am letzten End' die Seele mein[1]
    In Abrahams Schooss tragen;
    Den Leib in sein'm Schlafkämmerlein
    Gar sanft, ohn ein'ge Qual und Pein,
    Ruhn bis am jüngsten Tage!
    Alsdann vom Tod erwecke mich,
    Dass meine Augen sehen dich
    In aller Freud', O Gottes Sohn,
    Mein Heiland und[2] Genadenthron!
    Herr Jesu Christ, erhöre mich,
    Ich will dich preisen ewiglich!
                 B.G. xii. (1) 131.

English translations of the Hymn are noted in the *Dictionary of Hymnology*, pp. 1004, 1648.

Form. Simple (2 *Fl.*, 2 *Ob.*, *Strings*, *Organ, and Continuo*)[3].

[1] 1571 An meinem End mein Seelelein.
[2] 1571 und mein.
[3] Appendix A of the Bach-Gesellschaft Full-Score is a movement (Arie und Choral), in which the 33rd stanza (Jesu, deine Passion Ist mir lauter Freude) of Paul Stockmann's "Jesu Leiden, Pein und Tod" is set to Melchior Vulpius' melody (see No. 11 *supra*). The movement was discarded by Bach in the later versions of the Oratorio.

THE CHRISTMAS ORATORIO
(1734)

No. 5. How shall I fitly meet thee[1]
(*Wie soll ich dich empfangen*)

For Hans Hassler's melody, "Herzlich thut mich verlangen," see the "St Matthew Passion," No. 21 *supra*.

The words of the Choral are the first stanza of Paul Gerhardt's (see "St Matthew Passion," No. 16) Advent Hymn, "Wie soll ich dich empfangen," founded on St Matthew xxi. 1–9, and presumably written during the Thirty Years' War. It was first printed in Christoph Runge's *D. M. Luthers Und anderer vornehmen geistreichen und gelehrten Männer Geistliche Lieder und Psalmen*, Berlin, 1653, to which Johann Crüger contributed a melody for Gerhardt's Hymn:

    Wie soll ich dich empfangen,
    Und wie begegn' ich dir?
    O aller Welt Verlangen,
    O meiner Seelen Zier!
    O Jesu, Jesu! setze
    Mir selbst die Fackel bei,
    Damit, was dich ergötze,
    Mir kund und wissend sei.   B.G. v. (2) 36.

[1] The English titles are from the Rev. J. Troutbeck's version, published by Novello & Co.

English translations of the Hymn are noted in the *Dictionary of Hymnology*, p. 1280.

Form. Simple (1 *Fl.*, 2 *Ob.*, Strings, Organ, and *Continuo*).

No. 7. For us to earth he cometh poor
(*Er ist auf Erden kommen arm*)

Melody: "*Gelobet seist du, Jesu Christ*"　　Anon. 1524

The melody, "Gelobet seist du, Jesu Christ," a tune clearly derived from a pre-Reformation source, was published at Wittenberg in 1524 by Johann Walther in his collection of 32 hymns and 38 melodies, mostly in five parts, under the title *Geystliche gesangk Buchleyn*. Johann Walther was born in Thuringia in 1496, and, after serving as Sängermeister at Torgau, was appointed (1548) Kapellmeister at Dresden by the Elector Maurice of Saxony. He held the post until 1554, and returning to Torgau died there in 1570. In 1524 he spent three weeks with Luther at Wittenberg, along with Conrad Rupff, fitting tunes, old and new, to Luther's hymns for the *Geystliche gesangk*

Buchleyn. "Gelobet seist du" probably is his handiwork.

Bach uses the melody elsewhere in No. 28 of the "Christmas Oratorio," and in the Christmas Cantatas, "Sehet! welch' eine Liebe hat uns der Vater erzeiget" (No. 64), and "Gelobet seist du, Jesu Christ" (No. 91). Another harmonisation of the tune is in the *Choralgesänge*, No. 107.

The words of the Choral are the sixth stanza of Luther's Christmas Hymn, "Gelobet seist du, Jesu Christ," a version of the Latin sequence "Grates nunc omnes reddamus," first published in broadsheet form at Wittenberg in 1524, and (to the melody) in Walther's *Buchleyn*:

> Er ist auf Erden kommen arm,
> Dass er unser sich erbarm',
> Uns in[1] dem Himmel mache reich,
> Und seinen lieben Engeln gleich.
>   Kyrieleis!
>   B.G. v. (2) 37.

English translations of the Hymn are noted in the *Dictionary of Hymnology*, p. 408.

Form. Five unison (*Soprano*) phrases interrupted by Bass *Recitativo* (1 *Ob.*, 1 *Ob. d'amore*, 1 *Fagotto, Organ, and Continuo*).

[1] 1524 Und nun.

44 CHRISTMAS ORATORIO

No. 9. Ah! dearest Jesus, holy Child
(*Ach, mein herzliebes Jesulein!*)

Melody: "*Vom Himmel hoch*" ? Martin Luther 1539

The melody, "Vom Himmel hoch," with probability attributed to Martin Luther, was first published (Leipzig, 1539) in the *Geistliche lieder auffs new gebessert* of the Leipzig bookseller, Valentin S. Schumann (d. 1545), with the Hymn.

The melody is used by Bach in the "Christmas Oratorio" three times (Nos. 9, 17, 23), and in two cases (Nos. 9 and 23) is ornamented by stately orchestral interludes. It will be noticed that Bach employs in No. 9 the same orchestral tone as in No. 1, while the brilliant trumpet and tympani interludes in both are similar in design. Thereby he imposes upon the First Part of the Oratorio a clear impression of unity. Bach wrote a four-part arrangement of the melody which was sung at Christmas (1723) after the *Et exultavit spiritus meus* in the five-part "Magnificat[1]."

---

[1] It is printed as No. 298 of Ludwig Erk's *Choralgesänge und geistliche Arien* (Peters), 2 vols., 1850–65.

The words of the Choral are the thirteenth stanza of Luther's Christmas Hymn, "Vom Himmel hoch da komm ich her," which first appeared in the Wittenberg printer Joseph Klug's *Geistliche Lieder*, published at Wittenberg in 1535, but to the melody of the riddle-song, "Aus fremden Landen komm ich her," whose ribald associations compelled its abandonment for that of 1539:

> Ach, mein herzliebes Jesulein!
> Mach' dir ein rein sanft Bettelein,
> Zu ruh'n in meines Herzens Schrein,
> Dass ich nimmer vergesse dein.
>
> B.G. v. (2) 47.

English translations of the Hymn are noted in the *Dictionary of Hymnology*, pp. 1227, 1722.

Form. Extended (3 *Trombe, Timpani,* 2 *Fl.,* 2 *Ob.,* 1 *Fagotto, Strings, Organ, and Continuo*).

No. 12. BREAK FORTH, O BEAUTEOUS HEAVENLY LIGHT (*Brich an, O schönes Morgenlicht*)

Melody: "*Ermuntre dich, mein schwacher Geist*"
Johann Schop 1641

The melody, "Ermuntre dich, mein schwacher Geist," was composed by Johann Schop (see the "St Matthew Passion," No. 48), and appeared in Part I. of Johann Rist's *Himlischer Lieder mit Melodeien*, published at Lüneburg in 1641. Bach follows Johann Crüger's remodelling of the melody in the 1648 edition of his *Praxis Pietatis Melica*.

Bach uses the melody in two of the Cantatas, in both cases in ¾ measure: "Gott fähret auf mit Jauchzen" (No. 43), for Ascensiontide; and in the "Ascension Oratorio," "Lobet Gott in seinen Reichen" (No. 11).

The words of the Choral are the ninth stanza of Johann Rist's (see the "St Matthew Passion," No. 48) Christmas Hymn, "Ermuntre dich, mein schwacher Geist," founded on Isaiah ix. 2-7. It was first published, with the tune, in the first Part of Johann Rist's *Himlischer Lieder*, at Lüneburg in 1641:

> Brich an, O[1] schönes Morgenlicht,
> Und lass den Himmel tagen!
> Du Hirtenvolk, erschrecke nicht,
> Weil dir die Engel sagen:
> Dass dieses schwache Knäbelein
> Soll unser Trost und Freude sein,
> Dazu den Satan zwingen
> Und letztlich Frieden bringen.
>
> B.G. v. (2) 59.

---

[1] 1641 du.

Translations of the Hymn into English are noted in the *Dictionary of Hymnology*, p. 965.

Form. Simple (2 *Fl.*, 2 *Ob. d'amore*, 2 *Ob. da caccia*, *Strings*, *Organ*, *and Continuo*).

NO. 17. WITHIN YON GLOOMY MANGER (*Schaut hin! dort liegt*)

For the melody, "Vom Himmel hoch," see No. 9 *supra*.

The words of the Choral are the eighth stanza of Paul Gerhardt's (see the "St Matthew Passion," No. 16) Christmas Hymn, "Schaut! schaut! was ist für Wunder dar?" It was first published in the fifth "Dozen" of Johann G. Ebeling's (see No. 33 *infra*) edition of Gerhardt's *Geistliche Andachten*, Berlin, 1667:

> Schaut hin! dort liegt im finstern Stall,
> Dess' Herrschaft gehet überall.
> Da Speise vormals sucht' ein Rind,
> Da ruhet jetzt der Jungfrau'n Kind.
> B.G. v. (2) 66.

A translation of the Hymn is noted in the *Dictionary of Hymnology*, p. 411.

Form. Simple (2 *Fl.*, 2 *Ob. d'amore*, 2 *Ob. da caccia*, *Strings*, *Organ*, *and Continuo*).

No. 23. WITH ALL THY HOSTS (*Wir singen dir*)

For the melody, "Vom Himmel hoch," see No. 9 *supra*.

As in the First Part, Bach is at pains to link the concluding number of the Second Part (No. 23) with its opening one (No. 10) by weaving into it the rhythm and subject of the Pastoral Symphony (No. 10). The employment of the same tune for the concluding number of both Parts also, no doubt, was intentional; for their action is simultaneous—the birth of Christ in Part One and its announcement to the shepherds in Part Two.

The words of the Choral are the second stanza of Paul Gerhardt's (see the "St Matthew Passion," No. 16) Christmas Hymn, "Wir singen dir, Immanuel," which was first published in Johann Crüger's *Praxis Pietatis Melica*, Berlin, 1653:

> Wir singen dir in deinem Heer
> Aus aller Kraft: Lob, Preis und Ehr',
> Dass du, O lang gewünschter Gast,
> Dich nunmehr eingestellet hast.
> B.G. v. (2) 90.

English translations of the Hymn are noted in the *Dictionary of Hymnology*, p. 1288.

Form. Extended (2 *Fl.*, 2 *Ob. d'amore*, 2 *Ob. da caccia, Strings, Organ, and Continuo*).

No. 28. THE LORD HATH ALL THESE WONDERS WROUGHT (*Dies hat er Alles uns gethan*)

For the melody, "Gelobet seist du," see No. 7 *supra*.

The words of the Choral are the seventh and last stanza of Luther's Hymn, "Gelobet seist du, Jesu Christ" (see No. 7):

> Dies hat er Alles uns gethan,
> Sein' gross' Lieb' zu zeigen an;
> Dess freu' sich alle Christenheit,
> Und dank' ihm dess in Ewigkeit.
> Kyrieleis!
> B.G. v. (2) 110.

Form. Simple (2 *Fl.*, 2 *Ob.*, *Strings*, *Organ*, and *Continuo*).

No. 33. THEE WITH TENDER CARE I'LL CHERISH (*Ich will dich mit Fleiss bewahren*)

Melody: "*Warum sollt' ich mich denn grämen*"
Johann Georg Ebeling 1666

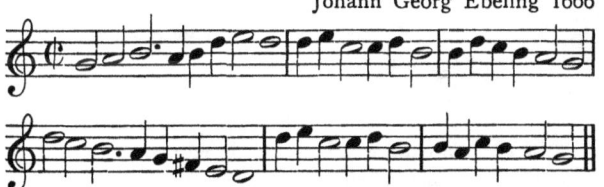

The melody, "Warum sollt' ich," was composed by Johann Georg Ebeling and was first published in his *Geistliche Andachten*, Berlin, 1666, the first collection of Gerhardt's Hymns, issued in 10 "Dozens" in 1666–67. Bach uses only the first half of the melody and, except in the second half of his fourth and first half of his fifth bars, follows Daniel Vetter's reconstruction (*Musicalische Kirch- und Hauss-Ergötzlichkeit*, Leipzig, Pt II., 1713) of Ebeling's tune. Ebeling was born at Lüneburg in 1637. He became Director of the Music at the Church of St Nicolas, Berlin, in 1662, and in 1668 was appointed Professor of Music in the Caroline Gymnasium at Stettin. He died at Stettin in 1676.

Bach uses the melody in the Motett, "Fürchte dich nicht." See also the *Choralgesänge*, No. 334.

The words of the Choral are the fifteenth and last stanza of Paul Gerhardt's (see the "St Matthew Passion," No. 16) Christmas Hymn, "Fröhlich soll mein Herze springen." It was first published in *Praxis Pietatis Melica* (Berlin, 1653), to a melody by Johann Crüger:

> Ich will dich mit Fleiss bewahren,
> Ich will dir
> Leben hier,
> Dir will ich abfahren.
> Mit dir will ich endlich schweben
> Voller Freud',
> Ohne Zeit
> Dort im andern Leben.
>
> B.G. v. (2) 124.

English translations of the Hymn are noted in the *Dictionary of Hymnology*, p. 397.

Form. Simple (2 *Fl.*, 2 *Ob.*, *Strings, Organ, and Continuo*).

NO. 35. REJOICE, AND SING (*Seid froh, dieweil*)

Melody: "*Wir Christenleut'*"

Caspar Fuger the younger 1593

The melody, "Wir Christenleut'," was published in Martin Fritzsch's *Gesangbuch. Darinnen Christliche Psalmen unnd Kirchen Lieder D. Martini Lutheri und andrer frommen Christen*, Dresden, 1593. It is one of seven new melodies in that collection, and may be attributed to the son of the author of the Hymn, "Wir Christenleut'," Caspar Fuger, or Füger, first published in the *Drey schöne Newe Geistliche Gesenge* (1592). Tune and hymn are found together in MS. 1589. Two Lutheran pastors, apparently father and son, named Caspar Fuger, or Füger, lived at Dresden in the sixteenth century. The authorship of the words of "Wir Christenleut'" has been attributed to both of them. The elder was Court Preacher and died *circ.* 1592. The younger was co-Rector of the Kreuzschule and died in 1617. In his *Christliche Verss und Gesenge* (Dresden, 1580) the elder Fuger states that his son had composed (in five parts) the music for his Hymns.

Bach uses the melody elsewhere in the Christmas Cantatas "Dazu ist erschienen der Sohn Gottes" (No. 40), "Unser Mund sei voll Lachens" (No. 110), and "Uns ist ein Kind geboren" (No. 142).

The words of the Choral are stated by the *Choralgesänge* (No. 381), following Erk, to be the second stanza of "Wir Christenleut'" *stark veränderte*. This, however, is not the case. The second stanza of "Wir Christenleut'" is as follows:

> Ein Wunder fremdt:
> Gott selbst wird heut
> Ein wahrer Mensch von Marie geboren.
> Ein Jungfrau zart
> Sein Mutter ward
> Von Gott dem Herren selbst dazu erkoren.

The words Bach uses here are these:

> Seid froh, dieweil
> Dass euer Heil
> Ist hie[1] ein Gott und auch ein Mensch geboren,
> Der welcher ist
> Der Herr und Christ
> In Davids Stadt, von Vielen auserkoren.
>   B.G. v. (2) 126.

[1] 1653 heut.

They are the fourth stanza of the Hymn "Lasst Furcht und Pein Fern von euch seyn," by Christoph Runge, published in Johann Crüger's *Praxis Pietatis Melica* (Berlin, 1653). Runge was born at Berlin in 1619, was in business as a printer there, and died in 1681.

Bach's choice of a stanza here was circumscribed. The text of No. 34 compelled him to treat Choral No. 35 as the utterance of the returning shepherds "praising and glorifying God for all the things which they had heard and seen." Runge's stanza, with its opening "Seid froh," exactly fits the situation. So also, it may be observed, does the fifth stanza of Fuger's Hymn, which begins, "Alleluja! gelobt sei Gott!"

Form. Simple (2 *Fl.*, 2 *Ob.*, *Strings*, *Organ*, *and Continuo*).

Nos. 38 & 40. Jesus, thou that for me livest (*Jesu du, mein liebstes Leben*) Jesu, thou my joy and pleasure (*Jesu, meine Freud' und Wonne*)

In both movements the Soprano *Arioso* is a *quasi* Choral tune, by Bach himself and, like No. 42 *infra*, obviously derived from No. 36 of this Oratorio. The words of the two movements together form the first stanza of Johann Rist's (see the "St Matthew Passion," No. 48) Hymn, "Jesu,

54 CHRISTMAS ORATORIO

du mein liebstes Leben," first published in 1642 in Part v. of his *Himlischer Lieder* (Lüneburg):

> (38) Jesu du, mein liebstes Leben,
> Meiner Seelen Bräutigam,
> Der du dich für mich gegeben
> An des bittern Kreuzes Stamm!
>
> (40) Jesu, meine Freud' und Wonne,
> Meine[1] Hoffnung, Schatz und Theil,
> Mein Erlöser, Schutz und Heil[2],
> Hirt und König, Licht und Sonne!
> Ach, wie soll ich würdiglich,
> Mein Herr Jesu, preisen dich?
> B.G. v. (2) 150, 158.

Form (both movements). A Soprano *Arioso* accompanying a Bass *Recitativo* (*Strings, Organ, and Continuo*).

NO. 42. JESUS WHO DIDST EVER GUIDE ME (*Jesus richte mein Beginnen*)

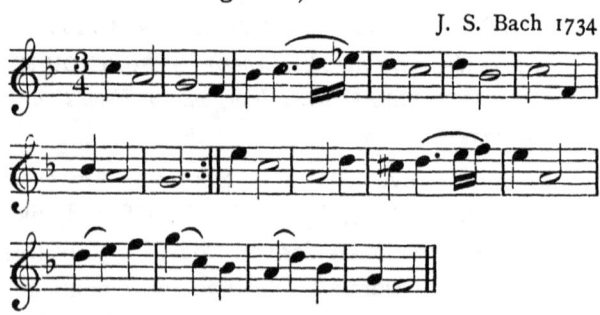

J. S. Bach 1734

---

[1] 1642 All mein.
[2] 1642 Mein Erlösung, Schmuck und Heil.

NUMBER 42

As in Parts I, II, and III Bach rounds off Part IV by connecting its opening and closing movements (Nos. 36 and 42). He does so in this case by inventing a melody, an *Aria* rather than a hymn-tune (*cf.* the concluding Choral of the Motett "Komm, Jesu, komm"), clearly derived from the Chorus "Come and thank Him" (No. 36), and by repeating the orchestral colour of that number.

The words of the Choral are the fifteenth stanza of Johann Rist's (see the "St Matthew Passion," No. 48) New Year Hymn, "Hilf, Herr Jesu, lass gelingen," first published in the third Part of Rist's *Himlischer Lieder*, Lüneburg, 1642:

> Jesus richte mein Beginnen,
> Jesus bleibe stets bei mir;
> Jesus zäume mir die Sinnen,
> Jesus sei nur mein' Begier.
> Jesus sei mir in Gedanken,
> Jesu, lasse mich nicht[1] wanken!
> B.G. v. (2) 166.

English translations of the Hymn are noted in the *Dictionary of Hymnology*, p. 523.

Form. Extended (2 *Corni*, 2 *Ob.*, *Strings*, *Organ, and Continuo*).

---

[1] 1642 nie mich.

No. 46. All darkness flies (*Dein Glanz all' Finsterniss verzehrt*)

For Seth Calvisius' melody, "In dich hab' ich gehoffet, Herr," see the "St Matthew Passion," No. 38.

The words of the Choral are the sixth and last stanza of Georg Weissel's Hymn, "Nun liebe Seel', nun ist es Zeit." Weissel was born at Domnau in 1590, and in 1623 became pastor of the newly built Altrossgart Church at Königsberg. He held the post until his death in 1635. He was one of the best of the early Prussian hymn-writers. His writings were published in the *Preussischen Festlieder* (Pt I., Elbing, 1642; Pt II., Königsberg, 1644). The Hymn, "Nun liebe Seel'," appeared in Pt I. of the *Festlieder*:

> Dein Glanz all' Finsterniss verzehrt,
> Die trübe Nacht in Licht verkehrt.
> Leit' uns auf[1] deinen Wegen,
> Dass dein Gesicht
> Und herrlich's Licht
> Wir ewig schauen mögen!
>
> B.G. v. (2) 190.

Form. Simple (2 *Ob. d'amore, Strings, Organ, and Continuo*).

---

[1] 1642 in.

Numbers 46 and 53

No. 53. This proud heart within us swelling (*Zwar ist solche Herzensstube*)

Melody: "*Gott des Himmels und der Erden*"
Heinrich Albert 1642

The melody, "Gott des Himmels und der Erden," was composed by Heinrich Albert, or Alberti, for the Hymn, of whose words also he was the author. He was born at Lobenstein in 1604, and in 1631 became organist of Königsberg Cathedral. He died at Königsberg in 1651. He published in eight Parts his *Arien oder Melodeyen Etlicher theils Geistlicher theils Weltlicher* (Königsberg, 1638–50). The Hymn "Gott des Himmels" was first published in Part V. of that collection in 1642. For all but the last two bars (which are closer to the Darmstadt *Cantional* of 1687) Bach gives the tune (with modifications necessitated by the rhythm of the words) as it appears in Daniel Vetter's Leipzig Hymn-Book (1713).

Bach has not used the melody elsewhere.

58 CHRISTMAS ORATORIO

The words of the Choral are the ninth stanza of Johann Franck's Morning Hymn, "Ihr Gestirn, ihr hohlen Lüfte." Franck was born at Guben in 1618, educated at Königsberg, became a lawyer, Burgomaster of Guben, and its representative in the Landtag of Lower Lusatia. He died in 1677. His hymns, 110 in number, were collected in his *Geistliches Sion* (Guben, 1674):

> Zwar ist solche Herzensstube
> Wohl kein schöner Fürstensaal,
> Sondern eine finstre Grube;
> Doch, sobald dein Gnadenstrahl
> In dieselbe nur wird blinken,
> Wird sie voller Sonnen dünken.
>   B.G. v.(2) 208.

Form. Simple (2 *Ob. d'amore, Strings, Organ, and Continuo*).

No. 59. BESIDE THY CRADLE HERE I STAND
(*Ich steh' an deiner Krippen hier*)

Melody: "*Nun freut euch, lieben Christen g'mein*"
                                    Anon. 1535

The melody bears the name of Luther's first congregational Hymn, "Nun freut euch, lieben Christen g'mein," and is said to have been written down by Luther after hearing a travelling artisan sing it. The tune was first published in the Wittenberg printer Joseph Klug's *Geistliche Lieder* (Wittenberg, 1535), and is generally known as "Luther's Hymn." An earlier melody to which the Hymn was sung appeared in the so-called *Achtliederbuch*, the small collection of eight hymns (along with four melodies) entitled *Etlich Christlich lider Lobgesang, und Psalm* (Wittenberg, 1524). The tune is familiar as No. 293 of *Hymns Ancient and Modern*, and is No. 261 of the *Choralgesänge*[1]. Both melodies are improbably attributed to Luther.

Bach has not used either melody in the Cantatas. There is another harmonisation of the 1535 tune in the *Choralgesänge*, No. 262, where it is set to a stanza of Bartholomäus Ringwaldt's Advent Hymn, "Es ist gewisslich an der Zeit," whose proper melody (1588) bears a close resemblance to it.

The words of the Choral are the first stanza of Paul Gerhardt's (see the "St Matthew Passion," No. 16) Christmas Hymn, "Ich steh' an deiner

---

[1] Erk, *op. cit.*, No. 272, prints the same version in A major.

Krippen hier," which was first published in Johann Crüger's *Praxis Pietatis Melica*, Berlin, 1653:

> Ich steh' an deiner Krippen hier,
> O Jesulein, mein Leben,
> Ich komme, bring' und schenke dir,
> Was du mir hast gegeben.
> Nimm hin, es ist mein Geist und Sinn,
> Herz, Seel' und Muth, nimm Alles hin,
> Und lass dir's wohl gefallen!
> B.G. v. (2) 245.

English translations of the Hymn are noted in the *Dictionary of Hymnology*, p. 410.

Form. Simple (2 *Ob.*, *Strings*, *Organ*, and *Continuo*).

No. 64. NOW VENGEANCE HATH BEEN TAKEN
(*Nun seid ihr wohl gerochen*)

For Hans Hassler's melody, "Herzlich thut mich verlangen," see the "St Matthew Passion," No. 21 *supra*.

The words of the Choral are the fourth stanza of Georg Werner's Hymn, "Ihr Christen auserkoren." Werner was born in 1589 at Preussisch-Holland, near Elbing. In 1614 he became master in a school at Königsberg, and in 1621 was appointed deacon of the Löbenicht Church there. He died at Königsberg in 1643. He edited the

New Preussisches vollständiges Gesangbuch (Königsberg, 1650 [1643]), and contributed Hymns to Bernhard Derschau's *Ausserlesene Geistliche Lieder*, Königsberg, 1639. The Hymn "Ihr Christen auserkoren" was published in Johann Crüger's *Praxis Pietatis Melica* (Berlin, 1647):

> Nun seid ihr wohl gerochen
> An eurer Feinde Schaar,
> Denn Christus hat zerbrochen
> Was euch zuwider war;
> Tod, Teufel, Sünd' und Hölle
> Sind ganz und gar geschwächt,
> Bei Gott hat seine Stelle
> Das menschliche Geschlecht.
>
> B.G. v. (2) 256.

Form. Extended (3 *Trombe, Timpani*, 2 *Ob., Strings, Organ, and Continuo*).

THE ASCENSION ORATORIO

(Cantata 11, *Lobet Gott in seinen Reichen*)
(*circ.* 1736)

NO. 6. NOW AT THY FEET CREATION LIES[1] (*Nun lieget alles unter dir*)

For Johann Schop's (see "St Matthew Passion," No. 48) melody, "Ermuntre dich, mein schwacher Geist," see the "Christmas Oratorio," No. 12.

The words of the Choral are the fourth stanza of Johann Rist's (see the "St Matthew Passion," No. 48) Eucharistic Hymn, "Du Lebensfürst, Herr Jesu Christ." It was first published in Rist's *Himlischer Lieder*, Pt I., Lüneburg, 1641:

>Nun lieget alles unter dir,
>Dich selbst nur ausgenommen;
>Die Engel müssen für und für
>Dir aufzuwarten kommen.
>Die Fürsten stehn auch auf der Bahn,
>Und sind dir willig unterthan;
>Luft, Wasser, Feu'r und Erden
>Muss dir zu Dienste werden.
>   B.G. ii. 32.

Form. Simple (2 *Fl.*, 2 *Ob.*, *Strings, Continuo*).

[1] The titles are those of Paul England's version (Novello & Co.).

No. 11. When will the night be over?
(*Wann soll es doch geschehen*)

Melody: "Von Gott will ich nicht lassen"

Anon. 1572 [1571]

* A syllable is wanting in the third period of the melody.

Melody: "Helft mir Gott's Güte preisen" Anon. 1575 [1569]

· The two melodies, "Von Gott will ich nicht lassen" and "Helft mir Gott's Güte preisen," have a common origin and are practically identical. Their source is the tune of the secular song "Ich ging einmal spazieren," to which Ludwig Helmbold (1532–98) wrote his Hymn "Von Gott"

c. 1563. In Joachim Magdeburg's *Christliche und Tröstliche Tischgesenge* (Erfurt, 1572 [1571]) the tune was printed in association with Helmbold's Hymn. In the same period Wolfgang Figulus (*c.* 1520–91), at that time Cantor in the Fürstenschule at Meissen, published two versions of the melody in his *Weynacht Liedlein* (Frankfort on the Oder, 1575 [1569]) in association with Paul Eber's (1511–69) Hymn, "Helft mir Gott's Güte preisen." The second of them was in four-part harmony, whose Tenor has been represented as the true melody. Carl von Winterfeld (*Der evangelische Kirchengesang*, i. 420) attributes the tune to Johann Eccard (1553–1611).

Bach uses the melody "Von Gott" in the putative and unfinished Cantata, "Lobt ihn mit Herz und Munde," and in the Cantatas, "Herr, wie du willt, so schick's mit mir" (No. 73), for the Third Sunday after Epiphany; and "Was willst du dich betrüben" (No. 107), for the Seventh Sunday after Trinity. In the *Choralgesänge* there are three other harmonisations of the tune, Nos. 324, 325, and 326. The melody "Helft mir" appears in the Cantatas "Herr Gott, dich loben, wir" (No. 16), for the Feast of the Circumcision; "Gottlob! nun geht das Jahr zu Ende" (No. 28), for Christmas; and "Sie werden euch in den Bann thun" (No. 183), for the Sixth Sunday after Easter.

The words of the Choral are the seventh and last stanza of Gottfried Wilhelm Sacer's Ascension Hymn, "Gott fähret auf gen Himmel." Sacer was born at Naumburg in 1635, and was educated at Jena University. He abandoned a military career for the law, settled at Wolfenbüttel in 1683 as Kammer-und-Amts-advocat, and died there in 1699. His Hymns, which he began to publish in 1661, were collected and posthumously issued (*Geistliche, liebliche Lieder*, Gotha, 1714):

>   Wann soll es doch geschehen,
>   Wann kömmt die liebe Zeit,
>   Dass ich ihn werde[1] sehen
>   In seiner Herrlichkeit?
>   Du Tag, wann wirst du sein,
>   Dass wir den Heiland grüssen,
>   Dass wir den Heiland küssen?
>   Komm, stelle dich doch ein!
>   B.G. ii. 40.

English translations of the Hymn are noted in the *Dictionary of Hymnology*, p. 984.

Form. Choral Fantasia (3 *Trombe, Timpani, 2 Fl., 2 Ob., Strings, Continuo*).

[1] 1714 wir ihn werden.

INDEX

OF FIRST LINES, MELODIES, AUTHORS, COMPOSERS, SOURCES.

NOTE. The letters M, J, C, A, stand respectively for the "St Matthew Passion," "St John Passion," "Christmas Oratorio," and "Ascension Oratorio." The numerals indicate the Number in the Oratorio. Biographical details will be found at the first entry after an author's name.

Ach, grosser König, gross zu allen Zeiten, J 15
Ach Herr, lass dein lieb' Engelein, J 37
Ach, mein herzliebes Jesulein! C 9
Agnus Dei qui tollis peccata mundi, M 1
Ah! dearest Jesus, Holy Child, C 9
Albert, or Alberti, Heinrich (1604–51), C 53
Albrecht, Margrave of Brandenburg-Culmbach (1522–57), M 31
All darkness flies before Thy face, C 46
"Aller Christen Leib-Stücke" (Leipzig, 1633), J 11
"Arien oder Melodeyen" (Königsberg, 1638–50), C 53
Attaignant, Pierre (1529), M 31
Aus fremden Landen komm ich her, C 9
"Ausserlesene Geistliche Lieder" (Königsberg, 1639), C 64
"Auszzug guter alter ün newer Teutscher liedlein" (Nürnberg, 1539), M 16
Bach, Johann Sebastian (1685–1750), C 42

Be near me, Lord, when dying, M 72
Befiehl du deine Wege, stanza i, M 53
Beschaffens Glück ist unversaumt, M 31
Beside Thy cradle here I stand, C 59
Bin ich gleich von dir gewichen, M 48
Break forth, O beauteous heavenly light, C 12
Brich an, O schönes Morgenlicht, C 12
Brunswick-Lüneburg, Elisabeth Duchess of, M 1
Calvin's Hymn Book (Strassburg, 1539), M 35
Calvisius (Kallwitz), Seth (1556–1615), M 38, J 12, C 46
"Cantional" (Darmstadt, 1687), C 53
"Cantional Oder Gesang-Buch Augsburgischer Confession"
   (Leipzig, 1627 and 1645), M 38, J 22
"Cantionale sacrum" (Gotha, 1648), J 28
"Christliche Kirchen-Ordnung" (Erfurt, 1542), M 1
"Christliche Psalmen unnd Kirchen Lieder" (Dresden, 1593),
   C 35
"Christliche und Tröstliche Tischgesenge" (Erfurt, 1572
   [1571]), M 31, A 11
"Christliche Verss und Gesenge" (Dresden, 1580), C 35
Christus der uns selig macht, stanza i, J 12; stanza viii,
   J 35; melody, J 12, J 35
Commit thy way to Jesus, M 53
Corvinus, Anton (1542), M 1
Crüger, Johann (1598–1662), M 3, M 16, M 21, M 25, M 53,
   M 55, J 4, J 15, C 5, C 12, C 23, C 33, C 59, C 64
Dachstein, Wolfgang (d. c. 1561), M 35
"Davids Himlische Harpffen" (Nürnberg, 1581), M 38
Decius, Nicolaus (d. 1541), M 1
Dein Glanz all' Finsterniss verzehrt, C 46
Dein Will' gescheh', Herr Gott, zugleich, J 5
Derschau, Bernhard (1639), C 64
"Devoti Musica Cordis" (Leipzig, 1630), M 3
Dies hat er Alles uns gethan, C 28
Dresden "Gesangbuch" (1593), C 35
"Drey schöne Newe Geistliche Gesenge" (1592), C 35

Du edles Angesichte, M 63
Du Lebensfürst, Herr Jesu Christ, stanza iv, A 6
Durch dein Gefängniss, Gottes Sohn, J 22
Ebeling, Johann Georg (1637–76), C 33, M 16, C 17
Eber, Paul (1511–69), A 11
Eccard, Johann (1553–1611), A 11
"Ein New Gesengbuchlen" (Jung Bunzlau, 1531), J 12
"Ein schön geistlich Gesangbuch" (Jena, 1609), J 11
Ein Wunder fremdt, C 35
En moy le secret pensement, M 35
Er ist auf Erden kommen arm, C 7
Er nahm Alles wohl in Acht, J 30
Erkenne mich, mein Hüter, M 21
Ermuntre dich, mein schwacher Geist, stanza ix, C 12;
    melody, C 12, A 6
Es ist gewisslich an der Zeit, C 59
Es sind doch selig alle, melody, M 35
"Etlich Christlich lider" (Wittenberg, 1524), C 59
Figulus, Wolfgang (c. 1520–91), A 11
For us to earth He cometh poor, C 7
"Form und Ordnung Gaystlicher Gesang und Psalmen"
    (Augsburg, 1533), M 38
Forster, Georg (1539), M 16
Franck, Johann (1618–77), C 53
Fritzsch, Martin (1593), C 35
Fröhlich soll mein Herze springen, stanza xv, C 33
"Fünff Schöne Geistliche Lieder" (Dresden, 1556), M 31
Fuger, Caspar (d. circ. 1592), C 35
Fuger, Caspar (d. 1617), C 35
"Geistlich Kleinod" (Leipzig, 1586), J 37
"Geistliche Andachten" (Berlin, 1666–67), M 16, C 17, C 33
"Geistliche, liebliche Lieder" (Gotha, 1714), A 11
"Geistliche Lieder" (Wittenberg, 1535), C 9, C 59
"Geistliche lieder" (Leipzig, 1539), M 1, J 5, C 9
"Geistliche Lieder und Psalmen" (Berlin, 1653), C 5
"Geistlicher Zeit-Vertreiber" (Leipzig, 1656), J 11

INDEX

"Geistliches Sion" (Guben, 1674), C 53
Gelobet seist du, Jesu Christ, stanza vi, C 7; stanza vii, C 28; melody, C 7, C 28
Gerhardt, Paul (1607-76), M 16, M 21, M 23, M 44, M 53, M 63, M 72, J 8, C 5, C 17, C 23, C 33, C 59
"Gesangbuch, Darinnen Psalmen unnd Geistliche Lieder" (Eisleben, 1598), M 16
"Geystliche gesangk Buchleyn" (Wittenberg, 1524), C 7
"Geystliche Lieder, Psalmen und Lobgesenge" (Nürnberg, 1569), M 16
"Geystlyke leder" (Rostock, 1531), M 1
Gott des Himmels und der Erden, melody, C 53
Gott fähret auf gen Himmel, stanza vii, A 11
Grates nunc omnes reddamus, C 7
Greitter, Matthäus (d. 1550 or 1552), M 35
Hammerschmidt, Andreas (1612-75), M 72 note
"Harmonia Cantionum ecclesiasticarum" (1598), J 12
"Harmoniae sacrae" (Görlitz, 1613), M 21
Hassler, Hans Leo (1564-1612), M 21, M 23, M 53, M 63, M 72, C 5, C 64
"Haus Kirchen Cantorei" (Bautzen, 1587), J 37
Heermann, Johann (1585-1647), M 3, M 25, M 55, J 4, J 15
Helft mir Gott's Güte preisen, melody, A 11
Helmbold, Ludwig (1532-98), A 11
Help us, Christ, Almighty Son, J 35
Herberger, Valerius (1562-1627), J 28
Herbert, Petrus (d. 1571), J 11
Here would I stand beside Thee, M 23
"Hertzens Andachten Geistlicher Gesänglein" (1631), M 3
Herzlich Lieb hab' ich dich, stanza iii, J 37; melody, J 37
Herzlich thut mich verlangen, melody, M 21, M 23, M 53, M 63, M 72, C 5, C 64
Herzliebster Jesu, was hast du verbrochen, stanza i, M 3; stanza iii, M 25; stanza iv, M 55; stanza vii, J 4; stanzas viii, ix, J 15; melody, M 3, M 25, M 55, J 4, J 15
Hesse, Johann (1490-1547), M 16

Heyden, Sebald (d. 1561), M 35
Hildebrandt, Johann (1656), J 11, J 28
Hilf, Herr Jesu, lass gelingen, stanza xv, C 42
"Himlischer Lieder mit Melodeien" (Lüneburg, 1641-42), M 48, C 12, C 38, C 40, C 42, A 6
How falsely doth the world accuse, M 38
How shall I fitly meet Thee, C 5
"Hymni sacri Latini et germanici" (Erfurt, 1594), M 38
Ich bin's, ich sollte büssen, M 16
Ich ging einmal spazieren, melody, A 11
Ich, ich und meine Sünden, J 8
Ich kann's mit meinen Sinnen nicht erreichen, J 15
Ich steh' an deiner Krippen hier, stanza i, C 59
Ich will dich mit Fleiss bewahren, C 33
Ich will hier bei dir stehen, M 23
Ihr Christen auserkoren, stanza iv, C 64
Ihr Gestirn, ihr hohlen Lüfte, stanza ix, C 53
Il me souffit de tous mes maulx, melody, M 31
In dich hab' ich gehoffet, Herr, stanza v, M 38 ; melody, M 38, C 46
In meines Herzens Grunde, J 28
In this Thy bitter Passion, M 63
In vain on Thy perfections, Lord, J 15
Innsbruck, ich muss dich lassen, M 16
Isaak, Heinrich (b. *circ.* 1440), M 16, M 44, J 8
Jesu, deine Passion, J 37 note
Jesu, der du warest todt, J 32
Jesu du, mein liebstes Leben, stanza i, C 38
Jesu Kreuz, Leiden und Pein, melody, J 11, J 30, J 32, J 37 note
Jesu Leiden, Pein und Tod, stanza x, J 11 ; stanza xx, J 30 ; stanza xxxiii, J 37 note ; stanza xxxiv, J 32
Jesu, meine Freud' und Wonne, C 40
Jesu Thou my joy and pleasure, C 40
Jesus Christus unser Herr, M 35
Jesus richte mein Beginnen, C 42

INDEX

Jesus, Thou that for me livest, C 38
Jesus, Thou who knewest death, J 32
Jesus who didst ever guide me, C 42
Keimann, Christian (1607-62), M 72 note
"Kirchen Geseng und Geistliche Lieder" (Leipzig, 1604), J 11
"Kirchengesenge Deudtsch" (Magdeburg, 1545), M 1
Klug, Joseph (1535), C 9, C 59
Knoll, Christoph (1563-1650), M 21
Komm heiliger Geist, M 35
Lamb of God, I fall before Thee, M 48
Lasst Furcht und Pein, stanza iv, C 35
Leipzig "Gesangbuch" (1682), J 11
Lord Jesus, Thy dear Angel send, J 37
"Lüneburgisches Gesangbuch" (1686), C 35
"Lustgarten Neuer Teutscher Gesäng" (Nürnberg, 1601), M 21
Luther, Martin (1483-1546), M 53, J 5, C 5, C 7, C 9, C 28, C 59
Mach's mit mir, Gott, nach deiner Güt', melody, J 22
Magdeburg, Joachim (*circ*. 1525-83), M 31, A 11
Mein G'müt ist mir verwirret, M 21
Meinen Jesum lass ich nicht, stanza vi, M 72 note
Mir hat die Welt trüglich gericht't, M 38
"Musicalische Kirch- und Hauss-Ergötzlichkeit" (Leipzig, 1713), C 33, C 53
My Saviour, why must all this ill befall thee? M 25
My sin it is which binds Thee, M 16
"New Catechismus Gesangbüchlein" (Hamburg, 1598 [1597]), M 16
"New Preussisches Gesangbuch" (Königsberg, 1650 [1643]), C 64
"Newe Symbola" (Nürnberg, 1571), J 37
"Newes vollkömliches Gesangbuch" (Berlin, 1640), M 3
Now at Thy feet creation lies, A 6
Now vengeance hath been taken, C 64
Nun danket alle Gott, M 3

Nun freut euch, lieben Christen g'mein, melody, C 59
Nun liebe Seel', nun ist es Zeit, stanza vi, C 46
Nun lieget alles unter dir, A 6
Nun seid ihr wohl gerochen, C 64
O blessed Jesu, how hast Thou offended? M 3
O Father, let Thy will be done, M 31
O grosse Lieb', O Lieb' ohn' alle Maasse, J 4
O Haupt voll Blut und Wunden, stanzas i, ii, M 63; stanza v, M 21; stanza vi, M 23; stanza ix, M 72
O hilf, Christe, Gottes Sohn, J 35
O Lamb of God most holy, M 1
O Lamm Gottes unschuldig, stanza i, M 1; melody, M 1
O Lord, who dares to smite Thee? M 44, J 8
O Man, thy grievous sin bemoan, M 35
O Mensch, bewein' dein' Sünde gross, stanza i, M 35; melody, M 35
O mighty King, eternal is Thy glory, J 15
O sacred Head, surrounded, M 63
O Welt, ich muss dich lassen, melody, M 16, M 44, J 8
O Welt, sieh' hier dein Leben, stanza iii, M 44, J 8; stanza iv, J 8; stanza v, M 16
O wondrous Love, that suffers this correction, M 55
O wondrous Love, whose depths no heart has sounded, J 4
Patris Sapientia, Veritas divina, melody, J 12, J 35
Peter, faithless, thrice denies, J 11
Petrus, der nicht denkt zurück, J 11
"Praxis Pietatis Melica" (Berlin, 1647), M 16, C 64; (Berlin, 1648), C 12; (Berlin, 1653), C 23, C 33, C 35, C 59; (Frankfort, 1656), M 21, M 53
"Preussischen Festlieder" (Elbing-Königsberg, 1642-44), C 46
"Psalmen, gebett und Kirchenübung" (Strassburg, 1526), M 35
Receive me, my Redeemer, M 21
Reinigius, Paschasius (1587), J 37
Reissner, or Reusner, Adam (1496-c. 1575), M 38

INDEX 73

Rejoice, and sing, C 35
Ringwaldt, Bartholomäus (1532–*circ.* 1600), C 59
Rist, Johann (1607–67), M 48, C 12, C 38, C 40, C 42, A 6
Runge, Christoph (1619–81), C 5, C 35
Sacer, Gottfried Wilhelm (1635–99), A 11
Salve caput cruentatum, M 21
Schalling, Martin (1532–1608), J 37
Schaut hin! dort liegt im finstern Stall, C 17
Schaut! schaut! was ist für Wunder dar? stanza viii, C 17
Schein, Johann Hermann (1586–1630), J 22
Schmidt, Bernhard (1577), J 37
Schop, or Schopp, Johann (d. *circ.* 1665), M 48, C 12, A 6
Schumann, Valentin S. (d. 1545), M 1, J 5, C 9
See the Lord of life and light, J 12
Seid froh, dieweil, C 35
Spangenberg, Johann (1545), M 1
Staden, Johann (1581–1634), M 3
Stockmann, Paul (1602?–36), J 11, J 30, J 32, J 37 note
"Strassburger Kirchen ampt" (Strassburg, 1525), M 35
Sunderreitter, Gregorius (1581), M 38
Teschner, Melchior (1614), J 28
"Teutsch Kircheampt mit lobgsengen" (Strassburg, 1525), M 35
The Lord hath all these wonders wrought, C 28
Thee with tender care I'll cherish, C 33
This proud heart within us swelling, C 53
Thy bonds, O Son of God Most High, J 22
Thy will, O Lord, be done, J 5
"Trente et quatre chansons musicales" (Paris, [1529]), M 31
Valet will ich dir geben, stanza iii, J 28 ; melody, J 28
Vater unser im Himmelreich, stanza iv, J 5 ; melody, J 5
Vetter, Daniel (1713), C 33, C 53
Vom Himmel hoch da komm ich her, stanza xiii, C 9 ; melody, C 9, C 17, C 23
Von Gott will ich nicht lassen, melody, A 11

74 INDEX

Vulpius, Melchior (1560?-1615), J 11, J 30, J 32, J 37 note
Walther, Johann (1496-1570), C 7, C 28
Wann soll es doch geschehen, A 11
Warum sollt' ich mich denn grämen, melody, C 33
Was ist die Ursach' aller solche Plagen? M 25
Was mein Gott will, das g'scheh' allzeit, stanza i, M 31;
    melody, M 31
Weisse, Michael (1480?-1534), J 12, J 35
Weissenfels "Gesangbuch," the (1714), J 11
Weissel, Georg (1590-1635), C 46
Wenn ich einmal soll scheiden, M 72
Wer hat dich so geschlagen, M 44, J 8
Werde munter, mein Gemüthe, stanza vi, M 48; melody,
    M 48
Werner, Georg (1589-1643), C 64
"Weynacht Liedlein" (Frankfort, 1575 [1569]), A 11
When will the night be over? A 11
While His parting spirit sinks, J 30
Why doth the Saviour languish? J 8
Wie soll ich dich empfangen, stanza i, C 5
Wie wunderbarlich ist doch diese Strafe! M 55
Wir Christenleut', wir Christenleut', stanza ii, C 35; melody,
    C 35
Wir singen dir, Immanuel, stanza ii, C 23
Wir singen dir in deinem Heer, C 23
With all Thy hosts, O Lord, we sing, C 23
Within our inmost being, J 28
Within yon gloomy manger lies, C 17
Wolder, David (1597), M 16
Zwar ist solche Herzensstube, C 53
"Zwey Bücher Einer Neuen Kunstlichen Tabulatur" (Strassburg, 1577), J 37

Music and Books published by Travis & Emery Music Bookshop:

Anon.: Hymnarium Sarisburiense, cum Rubricis et Notis Musicis.
Agricola, Johann Friedrich from Tosi: Anleitung zur Singkunst.
Bach, C.P.E.: edited W. Emery: Nekrolog or Obituary Notice of J.S. Bach.
Bateson, Naomi Judith: Alcock of Salisbury
Bathe, William: A Briefe Introduction to the Skill of Song
Bax, Arnold: Symphony #5, Arranged for Piano Four Hands by Walter Emery
Burney, Charles: The Present State of Music in France and Italy
Burney, Charles: The Present State of Music in Germany, The Netherlands ...
Burney, Charles: An Account of the Musical Performances ... Handel
Burney, Karl: Nachricht von Georg Friedrich Handel's Lebensumstanden.
Burns, Robert: The Caledonian Musical Museum ..The Best Scotch Songs. (1810)
Cobbett, W.W.: Cobbett's Cyclopedic Survey of Chamber Music. (2 vols.)
Corrette, Michel: Le Maitre de Clavecin
Crimp, Bryan: Dear Mr. Rosenthal ... Dear Mr. Gaisberg ...
Crimp, Bryan: Solo: The Biography of Solomon
d'Indy, Vincent: Beethoven: Biographie Critique
d'Indy, Vincent: Beethoven: A Critical Biography
d'Indy, Vincent: César Franck (in French)
Fischhof, Joseph: Versuch einer Geschichte des Clavierbaues. (Faksimile 1853).
Frescobaldi, Girolamo: D'Arie Musicali per Cantarsi. Primo & Secondo Libro.
Geminiani, Francesco: The Art of Playing the Violin.
Handel; Purcell; Boyce; Geene et al: Calliope or English Harmony: Volume First.
Häuser: Musikalisches Lexikon. 2 vols in one.
Hawkins, John: A General History of the Science and Practice of Music (5 vols.)
Herbert-Caesari, Edgar: The Science and Sensations of Vocal Tone
Herbert-Caesari, Edgar: Vocal Truth
Hopkins and Rimboult: The Organ. Its History and Construction.
Hunt, John: - see separate list of discographies at the end of these titles
Isaacs, Lewis: Hänsel and Gretel. A Guide to Humperdinck's Opera.
Isaacs, Lewis: Königskinder (Royal Children) A Guide to Humperdinck's Opera.
Kastner: Manuel Général de Musique Militaire
Lacassagne, M. l'Abbé Joseph : Traité Général des élémens du Chant.
Lascelles (née Catley), Anne: The Life of Miss Anne Catley.
Mainwaring, John: Memoirs of the Life of the Late George Frederic Handel
Malcolm, Alexander: A Treaty of Music: Speculative, Practical and Historical
Marx, Adolph Bernhard: Die Kunst des Gesanges, Theoretisch-Practisch
May, Florence: The Life of Brahms
May, Florence: The Girlhood Of Clara Schumann: Clara Wieck And Her Time.
Mellers, Wilfrid: Angels of the Night: Popular Female Singers of Our Time
Mellers, Wilfrid: Bach and the Dance of God
Mellers, Wilfrid: Beethoven and the Voice of God
Mellers, Wilfrid: Caliban Reborn - Renewal in Twentieth Century Music

Music and Books published by Travis & Emery Music Bookshop:
Mellers, Wilfrid: Darker Shade of Pale, A Backdrop to Bob Dylan
Mellers, Wilfrid: François Couperin and the French Classical Tradition
Mellers, Wilfrid: Harmonious Meeting
Mellers, Wilfrid: Le Jardin Retrouvé, The Music of Frederic Mompou
Mellers, Wilfrid: Music and Society, England and the European Tradition
Mellers, Wilfrid: Music in a New Found Land: ... ... American Music
Mellers, Wilfrid: Romanticism and the Twentieth Century (from 1800)
Mellers, Wilfrid: The Masks of Orpheus: ...... the Story of European Music.
Mellers, Wilfrid: The Sonata Principle (from c. 1750)
Mellers, Wilfrid: Vaughan Williams and the Vision of Albion
Panchianio, Cattuffio: Rutzvanscad Il Giovine
Pearce, Charles: Sims Reeves, Fifty Years of Music in England.
Playford, John: An Introduction to the Skill of Musick.
Purcell, Henry et al: Harmonia Sacra ... The First Book, (1726)
Purcell, Henry et al: Harmonia Sacra ... Book II (1726)
Quantz, Johann: Versuch einer Anweisung die Flöte trave rsiere zu spielen.
Rameau, Jean-Philippe: Code de Musique Pratique, ou Methodes.
Rastall, Richard: The Notation of Western Music.
Rimbault, Edward: The Pianoforte, Its Origins, Progress, and Construction.
Rousseau, Jean Jacques: Dictionnaire de Musique
Rubinstein, Anton : Guide to the proper use of the Pianoforte Pedals.
Sainsbury, John S.: Dictionary of Musicians. (1825). 2 vols.
Serré de Rieux, Jean de : Les dons des Enfans de Latone
Simpson, Christopher: A Compendium of Practical Musick in Five Parts
Spohr, Louis: Autobiography
Spohr, Louis: Grand Violin School
Tans'ur, William: A New Musical Grammar; or The Harmonical Spectator
Terry, Charles Sanford: Bach's Chorals – Parts 1, 2 and 3.
Terry, Charles Sanford: John Christian Bach
Terry, Charles Sanford: J.S. Bach's Original Hymn-Tunes for Congregational Use.
Terry, Charles Sanford: Four-Part Chorals of J.S. Bach. (German & English)
Terry, Charles Sanford: Joh. Seb. Bach, Cantata Texts, Sacred and Secular.
Terry, Charles Sanford: The Origins of the Family of Bach Musicians.
Tosi, Pierfrancesco: Opinioni de' Cantori Antichi, e Moderni
Tosi, Pierfrancesco: Observations on the Florid Song.
Van der Straeten, Edmund: History of the Violoncello, The Viol da Gamba ...
Van der Straeten, Edmund: History of the Violin, Its Ancestors... (2 vols.)
Walther, J. G. [Waltern]: Musicalisches Lexikon [Musikalisches Lexicon]
Zwirn, Gerald: Stranded Stories From The Operas

Travis & Emery Music Bookshop
17 Cecil Court, London, WC2N 4EZ, United Kingdom.
Tel. (+44) 20 7240 2129
© Travis & Emery 2009

Discographies by Travis & Emery:
Discographies by John Hunt.

1987: 978-1-906857-14-1: From Adam to Webern: the Recordings of von Karajan.
1991: 978-0-951026-83-0: 3 Italian Conductors and 7 Viennese Sopranos: 10 Discographies: Arturo Toscanini, Guido Cantelli, Carlo Maria Giulini, Elisabeth Schwarzkopf, Irmgard Seefried, Elisabeth Gruemmer, Sena Jurinac, Hilde Gueden, Lisa Della Casa, Rita Streich.
1992: 978-0-951026-85-4: Mid-Century Conductors and More Viennese Singers: 10 Discographies: Karl Boehm, Victor De Sabata, Hans Knappertsbusch, Tullio Serafin, Clemens Krauss, Anton Dermota, Leonie Rysanek, Eberhard Waechter, Maria Reining, Erich Kunz.
1993: 978-0-951026-87-8: More 20th Century Conductors: 7 Discographies: Eugen Jochum, Ferenc Fricsay, Carl Schuricht, Felix Weingartner, Josef Krips, Otto Klemperer, Erich Kleiber.
1994: 978-0-951026-88-5: Giants of the Keyboard: 6 Discographies: Wilhelm Kempff, Walter Gieseking, Edwin Fischer, Clara Haskil, Wilhelm Backhaus, Artur Schnabel.
1994: 978-0-951026-89-2: Six Wagnerian Sopranos: 6 Discographies: Frieda Leider, Kirsten Flagstad, Astrid Varnay, Martha Moedl, Birgit Nilsson, Gwyneth Jones.
1995: 978-0-952582-70-0: Musical Knights: 6 Discographies: Henry Wood, Thomas Beecham, Adrian Boult, John Barbirolli, Reginald Goodall, Malcolm Sargent.
1995: 978-0-952582-71-7: A Notable Quartet: 4 Discographies: Gundula Janowitz, Christa Ludwig, Nicolai Gedda, Dietrich Fischer-Dieskau.
1996: 978-0-952582-75-5: Leopold Stokowski (1882-1977): Discography and Concert Register
1996: 978-0-952582-76-2: Makers of the Philharmonia: 11 Discographies: Alceo Galliera, Walter Susskind, Paul Kletzki, Nicolai Malko, Issay Dobrowen, Lovro Von Matacic, Efrem Kurtz, Otto Ackermann, Anatole Fistoulari, George Weldon, Robert Irving.
1996: 978-0-952582-72-4: The Post-War German Tradition: 5 Discographies: Rudolf Kempe, Joseph Keilberth, Wolfgang Sawallisch, Rafael Kubelik, Andre Cluytens.
1996: 978-0-952582-73-1: Teachers and Pupils: 7 Discographies: Elisabeth Schwarzkopf, Maria Ivoguen, Maria Cebotari, Meta Seinemeyer, Ljuba Welitsch, Rita Streich, Erna Berger.
1996: 978-0-952582-75-5: Leopold Stokowski: Discography and Concert Listing.
1996: 978-0-952582-76-2: Makers of the Philharmonia: 11 Discographies Alceo Galliera, Walter Susskind, Paul Kletzki, Nicolai Malko, Issay Dobrowen, Lovro Von Matacic, Efrem Kurtz, Otto Ackermann, Anatole Fistoulari, George Weldon, Robert Irving.
1996: 978-0-952582-77-9: Tenors in a Lyric Tradition: 3 Discographies: Peter Anders, Walther Ludwig, Fritz Wunderlich.
1997: 978-0-952582-78-6: The Lyric Baritone: 5 Discographies: Hans Reinmar, Gerhard Huesch, Josef Metternich, Hermann Uhde, Eberhard Waechter.
1997: 978-0-952582-79-3: Hungarians in Exile: 3 Discographies: Fritz Reiner, Antal Dorati, George Szell.
1997: 978-1-901395-00-6: The Art of the Diva: 3 Discographies: Claudia Muzio, Maria Callas, Magda Olivero.
1997: 978-1-901395-01-3: Metropolitan Sopranos: 4 Discographies: Rosa Ponselle, Eleanor Steber, Zinka Milanov, Leontyne Price.
1997: 978-1-901395-02-0: Back From The Shadows: 4 Discographies: Willem Mengelberg, Dimitri Mitropoulos, Hermann Abendroth, Eduard Van Beinum.
1997: 978-1-901395-03-7: More Musical Knights: 4 Discographies: Hamilton Harty, Charles Mackerras, Simon Rattle, John Pritchard.
1998: 978-1-901395-95-2: More Giants of the Keyboard: 5 Discographies: Claudio Arrau, Gyorgy Cziffra, Vladimir Horowitz, Dinu Lipatti, Artur Rubinstein.

1998: 978-1-901395-94-5: Conductors On The Yellow Label: 8 Discographies: Fritz Lehmann, Ferdinand Leitner, Ferenc Fricsay, Eugen Jochum, Leopold Ludwig, Artur Rother, Franz Konwitschny, Igor Markevitch.

1998: 978-1-901395-96-9: Mezzo and Contraltos: 5 Discographies: Janet Baker, Margarete Klose, Kathleen Ferrier, Giulietta Simionato, Elisabeth Hoengen.

1999: 978-1-901395-97-6: The Furtwaengler Sound Sixth Edition: Discography and Concert Listing.

1999: 978-1-901395-98-3: The Great Dictators: 3 Discographies: Evgeny Mravinsky, Artur Rodzinski, Sergiu Celibidache.

1999: 978-1-901395-99-0: Sviatoslav Richter: Pianist of the Century: Discography.

2000: 978-1-901395-04-4: Philharmonic Autocrat 1: Discography of: Herbert Von Karajan [Third Edition].

2000: 978-1-901395-05-1: Wiener Philharmoniker 1 - Vienna Philharmonic and Vienna State Opera Orchestras: Discography Part 1 1905-1954.

2000: 978-1-901395-06-8: Wiener Philharmoniker 2 - Vienna Philharmonic and Vienna State Opera Orchestras: Discography Part 2 1954-1989.

2001: 978-1-901395-07-5: Gramophone Stalwarts: 3 Separate Discographies: Bruno Walter, Erich Leinsdorf, Georg Solti.

2001: 978-1-901395-08-2: Singers of the Third Reich: 5 Discographies: Helge Roswaenge, Tiana Lemnitz, Franz Voelker, Maria Mueller, Max Lorenz.

2001: 978-1-901395-09-9: Philharmonic Autocrat 2: Concert Register of Herbert Von Karajan Second Edition.

2002: 978-1-901395-10-5: Sächsische Staatskapelle Dresden: Complete Discography.

2002: 978-1-901395-11-2: Carlo Maria Giulini: Discography and Concert Register.

2002: 978-1-901395-12-9: Pianists For The Connoisseur: 6 Discographies: Arturo Benedetti Michelangeli, Alfred Cortot, Alexis Weissenberg, Clifford Curzon, Solomon, Elly Ney.

2003: 978-1-901395-14-3: Singers on the Yellow Label: 7 Discographies: Maria Stader, Elfriede Troetschel, Annelies Kupper, Wolfgang Windgassen, Ernst Haefliger, Josef Greindl, Kim Borg.

2003: 978-1-901395-15-0: A Gallic Trio: 3 Discographies: Charles Muench, Paul Paray, Pierre Monteux.

2004: 978-1-901395-16-7: Antal Dorati 1906-1988: Discography and Concert Register.

2004: 978-1-901395-17-4: Columbia 33CX Label Discography.

2004: 978-1-901395-18-1: Great Violinists: 3 Discographies: David Oistrakh, Wolfgang Schneiderhan, Arthur Grumiaux.

2006: 978-1-901395-19-8: Leopold Stokowski: Second Edition of the Discography.

2006: 978-1-901395-20-4: Wagner Im Festspielhaus: Discography of the Bayreuth Festival.

2006: 978-1-901395-21-1: Her Master's Voice: Concert Register and Discography of Dame Elisabeth Schwarzkopf [Third Edition].

2007: 978-1-901395-22-8: Hans Knappertsbusch: Kna: Concert Register and Discography of Hans Knappertsbusch, 1888-1965. Second Edition.

2008: 978-1-901395-23-5: Philips Minigroove: Second Extended Version of the European Discography.

2009: 978-1-901395-24-2: American Classics: The Discographies of Leonard Bernstein and Eugene Ormandy.

2010: 978-1-901395-25-9: Dirigenten der DDR: Conductors of the German Democratic Republic

Discography by Stephen J. Pettitt, edited by John Hunt:

1987: 978-1-906857-16-5: Philharmonia Orchestra: Complete Discography 1945-1987

Available from: Travis & Emery at 17 Cecil Court, London, UK. (+44) 20 7 240 2129. email on sales@travis-and-emery.com .

© Travis & Emery 2009

www.ingramcontent.com/pod-product-compliance
Lightning Source LLC
Chambersburg PA
CBHW062009070426
42451CB00008BA/330